Piero Sraffa – unorthodox economist (1898–1983)

Piero Sraffa – unorthodox economist (1898–1983)

A biographical essay

Jean-Pierre Potier

London and New York

First published 1987 by Presses Universitaires de Lyon
86 rue Pasteur, 69007 Lyon
Un Economiste non conformiste – Piero Sraffa (1898–1983): Essai biographique

Published 1991
by Routledge
11 New Fetter Lane, London EC4P 4EE

Simultaneously published in the USA and Canada
by Routledge
a division of Routledge, Chapman and Hall, Inc.
29 West 35th Street, New York, NY 10001

Translated by Bernard Hoepffner
Typeset in Times by Michael Mepham, Frome, Somerset
Printed and bound in Great Britain by
Biddles Ltd, Guildford and King's Lynn

British Library Cataloguing in Publication Data
Potier, Jean-Pierre *1949–*
Piero Sraffa: unorthodox economist (1898–1983): a biographical essay.
1. Economics
I. Title
330.155092

✓ ISBN 0–415–05959–3

Library of Congress Cataloging-in-Publication Data
Has been applied for

For Colette

Contents

Preface

Since the publication, in 1960, of a short essay entitled *Production of Commodities by Means of Commodities: Prelude to a Critique of Economic Theory*, written by Piero Sraffa, an Italian economist living in Cambridge, an exceptionally intense debate has been going on throughout the world of economics. Few books have given rise to so much controversy among twentieth-century economists.

Maurice Dobb was right to describe the work, on its publication, as an 'epoch-making book', for today a 'Sraffian' or 'neo-Ricardian' school, whose approach is based on the idea of 'surplus', seems to be gradually establishing itself in the economists' galaxy. Sraffa's book has been seen as the basis of a radical critique of the dominant neo-classical economic theory. The book was thought by some to contain a critique of Marxist theory, especially of the problem of 'value' and of what has come to be called 'transformation', although Sraffa, who never wrote much, remained almost silent on the subject of Marx.

It has thus been enthralling to reconstruct the career of this original thinker. Precise information about the life of Sraffa is scarce, and scattered in works belonging to very different fields. He is of course the man who undertook the long and exacting task of editing David Ricardo's *Works and Correspondence* and who published the *Production of Commodities by Means of Commodities*. But his status is not only that of an economist, albeit an original one; research about his life shows that there were many other facets to his personality. During his youth, Sraffa was a militant and a revolutionary journalist; then, for eleven years, he gave all the assistance he could to the great Marxist theorist and Italian Communist Party leader, Antonio Gramsci, who had been imprisoned by the Fascists. Such devotion entailed a good deal of risk, and is worth examining. Piero Sraffa was also a man of profound culture, with a wide range of interests, capable of participating in debates at a very high level about numerous philosophical and scientific questions.

Though the need for a detailed biography of Piero Sraffa is currently apparent, writing such a work might prove to be a treacherous task. Sraffa was not a public figure like John Maynard Keynes. He was very reserved about his past, his relations with friends and his judgments about contemporary personalities; he always had a tendency to minimize the importance of the help that he gave to various people. Moreover, he intensely disliked writing, and whenever he launched himself into the task, he always maintained the utmost brevity. To date, his work has remained rather unknown, partly because such essential features as his Cambridge lectures of 1928 to 1930 are still unpublished.

This short book about Piero Sraffa, the great intellectual who died in Cambridge on 3 September 1983, does not pretend to be a complete 'intellectual biography', the sort of synthesis that might be entitled *The Life and Work of Piero Sraffa*. As the Sraffa papers in Cambridge are inaccessible for the moment, and as a Collected Works has yet to be published, I had to be more modest in my aim. I have deliberately focused on Sraffa's relations with a number of the most important intellectuals of the twenties and thirties, and especially on his unshakable friendship with Antonio Gramsci.[1] During my search for details about Sraffa's life, about his friendships and about his intellectual exchanges, from his first years in northern Italy to his nearly silent retirement at Trinity College, I came across numerous enigmas, and the search was, at times, disconcerting. A large number of difficulties arose when I tried to reconstruct particular periods, to establish various important links. While the task was certainly fascinating, this research led only to an incomplete essay, open to future revision.

The text of this English edition is a revised version of the French original, the Italian edition prepared by Antonio A Santucci, director of the Centro di Studi Gramsciani in Rome, published by Editori Riuniti (1990). The opportunity to read unpublished letters scattered among various archives was extremely valuable to me while writing the book, and I would like to thank those who helped me in the course of my research: Giulio Sapelli at the GianGiacomo Feltrinelli Foundation in Milan, Mrs Elsa Fubini at the Gramsci Foundation in Rome and Mrs Estella Giordano at the Luigi Einaudi Foundation of Turin.[2]

While working on this book between 1984 and 1986, I benefited from the advice and encouragement of my colleagues and friends at the Faculté des Sciences Economiques et de Gestion of the Université Lumière-Lyon II, in the Centre Analyse, Epistémologie, Histoire and the Centre A. et L. Walras, in particular from Pierre Dockès and Daniel Dufourt. During the various trips I made to Italy, I benefited from the advice of Riccardo Bellofiore, Aurelio Macchioro and, later, Antonio A. Santucci to whom I would like to express my gratitude. Moreover, I would like to thank those colleagues who very kindly read the French edition and made a number of comments and criticisms, and more particularly Richard Arena, Christian Bidard, Peter Groenewegen, Serge Latouche and Carlo Panico; I also owe a particular debt to Jan Van Daal, who took the initiative in having this English translation published and helped me prepare the text. However, I alone am responsible for the weaknesses, mistakes and omissions which remain in the book.

J-P. P.

1 The formative years

THE SON OF AN EMINENT JURIST

Piero Sraffa was the only son of a wealthy Jewish family from Pisa. This small Tuscan town is not far from Livorno (Leghorn), where the ancestors of David Ricardo, also Jewish, had lived from the early seventeenth century until about 1680; they were traders in coral.[1] Sraffa's ancestors on his father's side had been merchants in Pisa for generations. His father, Angelo Sraffa, the son of Giuseppe Sraffa and Marianna Treves, was born there on 19 December 1865.[2] After completing his secondary education, Angelo Sraffa went to the University of Pisa in 1884. At that time, the work of the poet Giosuè Carducci (1835–1907), winner of the Nobel Prize for literature in 1906, reviver of the classical tradition, opponent of romanticism and Christianity, had an enormous influence on the intellectual and academic life of the city.[3] Piero's father was strongly attracted to Carducci's writings, and put together an extensive library devoted to the latter's work.[4] At the university, he studied mainly in the Law Faculty, then one of the best-known in Italy. Among his professors were Francesco Carrara, Filippo Serafini (1831–97), editor of the *Archivio Giuridico*,[5] and David Supino, who, with Serafini, founded the review *Diritto Commerciale*. However, his real teacher in law was undoubtedly Ludovico Mortara, who later abandoned university teaching to become, before the First World War, First President of the Court of Appeal in Rome, Minister of Justice and Senator.

In 1888, Angelo Sraffa defended his thesis in law, 'La rendita di cosa altrui', which was published the following year in the *Archivio Giuridico*. For a while he practised as a lawyer, but then decided to pursue an academic career. In 1894, he obtained a post as Professor of Commercial Law at the University of Macerata; two years later, he taught in Messina. In 1898, he became professor at the Law Faculty of Parma, where he stayed until 1913. By then, he had already published the works which were to establish his reputation as a leading expert on Italian commercial law: *La liquidazione delle società commerciali*,[6] *La lotta commerciale*,[7] and *Il fallimento delle società commerciali*.[8] Among the many students who attended his courses of lectures at the University of Parma, one was later to win particular fame when the Fascist regime hardened its position. This was Alfredo Rocco (1875–1935), author of the 'leggi fascistissime' of November 1926.

In 1897, in Courmayeur, near Aosta, Angelo Sraffa married Irma Tivoli, who came from a distinguished Jewish family in Turin. The couple went to live in Parma. Their only son, Piero, was born in Turin on 5 August 1898. Luigi L. Pasinetti has pointed out that the mother 'came from a particularly matriarchal family and had a strong influence on her son's education'.[9] As was usual among mothers of upper middle-class families in Piedmont, she was fluent in French, and it was her task to teach this language to her son. All his life, Piero Sraffa was deeply attached to his mother's strong personality, which may perhaps explain why he was a bachelor and why he is not known to have had any affairs.

In 1900, Angelo Sraffa published his famous *Commentario al Codice di commercio*,[10] and three years later, he founded the *Rivista del Diritto Commerciale*[11] with his friend Cesare Vivante (1855–1944), professor at Rome University; the review's platform was the 'renovation' and the 'systematization' of commercial law in Italy. The reputation of Piero's father was such that he was asked to occupy the chair of commercial law, jointly with Leone Bolaffio, at the newly established Università Commerciale Luigi Bocconi in Milan in November 1902. This private institution was founded and financed by Senator Ferdinando Bocconi, owner of the Alle Città d'Italia department stores, in memory of his son Luigi, who had died in the Italian defeat at Adoua, in Ethiopia, in 1896.

At Bocconi, Angelo Sraffa struck up a friendship with the economist Luigi Einaudi (1874–1961), a former pupil of Salvatore Cognetti de Martiis, who, in 1902, had obtained a post as professor 'extraordinary' at the Law Faculty of Turin. The Sraffa family then settled in Milan, from 1903 to 1913, a period during which Angelo Sraffa's occupation spread to a variety of fields. He was a member of the team that systematized the Law relating to companies (1905-06), and standardized maritime law (1910). The Italian government appointed him plenipotentiary delegate to the second Hague Conference, held in June–July 1912, for the harmonization of the laws relating to bills of exchange, promissory notes and cheques. He contributed to *Rivista delle Società Commerciali*, organ of the Associazione fra le Società Italiane per Azioni, whose headquarters were in Rome, under the direction, between 1911 and 1920, of Antonio Scialoja. Angelo Sraffa was politically a liberal democrat, without, however, belonging to the conservative camp; at the beginning of the First World War, he did not share the views of the Nationalists.

In 1913, he was awarded a chair in commercial law at the University of Turin, and the family moved to the capital of Piedmont. During the worst phase of the war, in 1917, Angelo Sraffa became Rector of the Luigi Bocconi Commercial University, and the family had to move back to Milan. The nine years during which he occupied this post were crucial in the history of the institution: in 1920, he founded the Institute of Economics named after Senator Ettore Bocconi; Einaudi was its director until 1923, and its co-director until 1926, with the statistician Giorgio Mortara (1885–1967), the son of Ludovico Mortara.[12] In 1923, Angelo Sraffa decided to launch a review of the institute, the *Annali di Economia*, which started the following year. He also took other important initiatives, such as instituting study grants which allowed students to go abroad, and creating the first students' residences. Very much in demand for his expertise in commercial law, he participated, between 1919 and 1922, in proceedings aimed at reforming commercial law, as vice-president of a ministerial commission under the presidency of Cesare Vivante. But this project could not be brought to a conclusion because the Fascists came to power. Angelo Sraffa was only a consultant to the new reform commission, set up in 1924, and presided over, this time, by an uncle of Piero's on his mother's side who will be referred to later in connection with Gramsci, namely Mariano D'Amelio (1871–1943).[13] In 1924, Piero's father was appointed president of the Law Faculty of the recently created State University of Milan.

During 1924–25 the repression of the opposition by the Fascist regime hardened; the regime also tightened its vigilance over the university establishments. In his memoirs, the economist Libero Lenti recalled one of the last examples of opposition at Bocconi: the memorable *viva* of Lelio Basso (1903–78). This young socialist was under arrest, though he was allowed, in June 1925, to defend his doctoral thesis on 'The conception of freedom in the works of Marx', whilst surrounded by policemen; the examiners, under Angelo Sraffa's presidency, gave him the highest marks *summa cum laude*.[14] In 1926, the Fascists made it impossible for Piero's father to keep his post as Rector of the Bocconi University although he stayed on as a member of the management committee until 1934, and edited the *Rivista del Diritto Commerciale*. He abandoned teaching to practise again as a lawyer. From 1925 he had been in charge of the 'Private Law' section of the famous *Enciclopedia Italiana*, financed by the industrialist Giovanni Treccani and directed by the Fascist philosopher Giovanni Gentile; he directed the work of a team of collaborators who wrote the papers. He retired to his villa, San Michele, in Rapallo and died on 10 December 1937; his wife survived him until 1945. The Institute of Comparative Law, founded in 1934–35 by Mario Rotondi at the Bocconi University, was later to take the name 'Angelo Sraffa Institute of Comparative, Commercial, Industrial and Employment Law', and was to be responsible for the publication of the *Rivista del Diritto Commerciale*.[15] Not far from the university, a square was to be given the name Angelo Sraffa after the Second World War.

INTELLECTUAL DEVELOPMENT WITHIN 'NEO-IDEALISM' WITH SOME SYMPATHY FOR SOCIALIST IDEAS

When the young Piero finished primary school in Parma, he went on to study 'grammar' at the famous Giuseppe Parini secondary school in Milan. He left this establishment in 1913 when his father was appointed to a chair in commercial law at Turin University and transferred to the prestigious Massimo D'Azeglio school, where he finished his secondary schooling in 1915 with the highest possible marks.

Like most young intellectuals of that time, his cultural background was dominated by 'neo-idealism' or neo-Hegelianism, represented by the thinking of Benedetto Croce (1866–1952) and Giovanni Gentile (1875–1944).[16] A liberal, secular thinker, and later an adversary of Fascism, Croce constructed, between 1900 and 1910, a historicist philosophy which was to be a 'science of the mind' based on a critical reading of Hegel.[17] Gentile, who started out as a liberal, but was later to become the theorist of Fascism, was also a critical disciple of Hegel and developed an 'actualist' philosophy that renewed links with the Italian and European spiritualist tradition. The young Piero read the journal published in Naples from 1903 by Croce, *La Critica: Rivista di letteratura, storia e filosofia*. His friend Antonio Gramsci, in a highly polemical paper of 1924, mentions Sraffa's 'democratic-liberal intellectual background, that is to say, normative and Kantian, non-Marxist and non-dialectical'.[18] Such an emphatic judgment naturally cannot be accepted without reservations.

Although he had been educated in the liberal tradition, Piero Sraffa had great sympathy with socialist ideas. His initiation in politics took place just at the end of the 'Giolitti era'; the President of the Council, Giovanni Giolitti (1842–1928), considered the architect of the alliance between the landowners of the South and the entrepreneur capitalists of the North, nevertheless succeeded in gradually integrating the masses into political life. At a very early age, in 1913, Piero Sraffa had been influenced by Domenico Re, a socialist teacher at the Parini school in Milan.[19] In Turin, at the Massimo D'Azeglio school, a former socialist, Umberto Cosmo (1868–1944) who taught Italian literature, a disciple of Croce in philosophy, and a Dante scholar, became interested in Piero. They had some fruitful discussions. Cosmo's personality was particularly interesting; he had joined the Italian Socialist Party in 1896, though he left it later for family reasons; before the First World War, although he did not agree with the 'revolutionary' wing dominating the Socialist Party since 1912, as represented, in particular, by Benito Mussolini, he strongly criticized the reformist socialism of Filippo Turati (1857–1932), which he described as the 'socialism of scoundrels'.[20] During the 1914 elections, Cosmo supported the Socialist candidate of the 'revolutionary' tendency and to this end he invited Gaëtano Salvemini (1873–1957), founder of the journal *L'Unità* in 1911, to Turin. Salvemini was a famous 'meridionalist' that is to say, a socialist opposed to the situation of the south of Italy as in effect a colony of the North; his policies were aimed at building an alliance between the small farmers of the South and the labourers of the North. In this way, Cosmo gained the sympathy of the young revolutionaries of Turin, assiduous readers of *L'Unità*, and the future founders of *L'Ordine Nuovo*. These young people included Angelo Tasca, Umberto Terracini and Gramsci, as well as Sraffa.[21] It is nevertheless difficult to ascertain the political and social opinions of the young Piero just before the outbreak of the First World War; however, without doubt it was his attraction to socialism that led him to become interested in economic questions at an early age.

THE FIRST WORLD WAR, UNIVERSITY STUDIES AND THE MEETING WITH ANTONIO GRAMSCI

In August 1914, war broke out with Italy taking no immediate part. The 'interventionists' were triumphant when, on 24 May 1915, Italy declared war on Austria. The Italian Socialist Party had defended the principle of neutrality, opposed the war and participated in the international conferences of Zimmerwald (1915) and of Kienthal (1916). The military campaign did not get off to a very auspicious start. Against the Austrians, on 25 October 1917, Italy sustained the terrible defeat of Caporetto. The same year, in February, revolution broke out in Tsarist Russia and, in November, the Bolsheviks came to power. The ideas of Sraffa became more radical after these events. In a letter that he wrote to Gramsci in 1924, he gave some indication of this change:

> I had settled, until 1917, into the pacifist socialism of 1914–15, from which I was shaken by the discovery, which I made after Caporetto and the November Russian Revolution, that the guns were precisely in the hands of the worker-soldiers. [22]

In autumn 1916, Piero Sraffa left secondary school and entered the Law Faculty at Turin, following the advice of his father, who did not want him to enrol at Milan. Among the courses available in political economy, he chose to follow those of Luigi Einaudi, specialist in financial science and friend of his father, as well as those of the marginalist Pasquale Jannaccone (1872–

1960), Professor of Statistics and disciple of Alfred Marshall. Both these economists worked at the Laboratorio di Economia Politica which had been founded at the faculty, in 1893, by the 'socialist of the chair', Salvatore Cognetti de Martiis (1844–1901), in order to stimulate an experimental and empirical approach. Sraffa does not appear to have been much attracted by the economic history teaching of the unorthodox Achille Loria (1857–1943). Loria had been educated within the context of the 'Lombard-Venetian school', comparable to the German historical school; he was anti-marginalist and the theorist of a strange agrarian socialism. The man who 'introduced' Karl Marx into Italy, Loria had had heated debates with Friedrich Engels about the 'transformation problem'.[23] It should be mentioned here that the majority of the economists at Turin at the time were influenced by the work of Alfred Marshall, in contrast to those at Rome, like Enrico Barone and Umberto Ricci, who were faithful to the ideas of Léon Walras and in particular to those of Vilfredo Pareto.[24] But Sraffa soon found himself unable to follow the courses in Turin, because, from 1917 to 1918, he had to do his military service. Among other things, he acted as a skiing instructor and, when posted to the Engineers, found himself having to blow up bridges to slow down the advance of the Austrian troops.[25] Towards the end of the war, he became an officer; he nevertheless managed to pass the university examinations in the Faculty of Jurisprudence.

At the end of 1918, finally freed from his military obligations, Sraffa returned to Turin and finished his legal studies. He wanted to make himself useful to the revolutionary movement, which was very active in the Piedmontese capital. Umberto Cosmo, who had been his teacher at the Massimo D'Azeglio school, did something which was to have enormous consequences for Sraffa's future political activities: he introduced him to Antonio Gramsci (1891–1937), most probably in 1919.[26] In March 1919, with the help of Angelo Tasca (1892–1960), Doctor of Literature, Umberto Terracini (1895–1983), Doctor of Law, and Palmiro Togliatti (1893–1964), Doctor of Law,[27] Gramsci had founded a weekly review situated at the extreme left of the Italian Socialist Party. *L'Ordine Nuovo: Rassegna settimanale di cultura socialista.* This journal started coming out on 1 May, and became the voice of the worker's council movement, which developed rapidly in the troubled circumstances of the time. Two outstanding but fruitless episodes must be mentioned in this respect: first the famous 'clock hands' strike of April 1920 in Turin,[28] and second the movement during which factories were occupied throughout Italy, in September 1920.[29]

Sraffa, immediately after having met Gramsci, decided to join the editorial team of *L'Ordine Nuovo*, and had friendly relations with the main journalists. According to the accounts of some colleagues, it appears that, in 1919 and 1920, he made several translations of German, French and English texts.[30]

He was also active in the Socialist Students' Group (*Gruppo studentesco socialista*), created in Turin at Gramsci's instigation, at the beginning of 1920. This circle, made up of students and former students, defended a political position that was very close to that of *L'Ordine Nuovo*, during weekly meetings at the Trade Union Centre of Turin.[31] The crisis of Italian socialism, especially after the failure of the movement to occupy the factories, led to the constitution of the Italian Communist Party at the Congress of Livorno in january 1921. Before examining, in the following chapter, the relationship between Sraffa, Gramsci and the Communists in the twenties and thirties, before and after his move to Cambridge, it is necessary to look back at his education and other activities.

THE DOCTORAL THESIS AND THE FIRST STUDY TRIP TO BRITAIN

In the period 1919 to 1920, Sraffa was working on a doctoral thesis in economics under the supervision of Einaudi, who had just become a Senator. The subject he had chosen was topical, as appears from the definitive title of the work: *L'inflazione monetaria in Italia durante e dopo la guerra.*[32] The work reveals a profound knowledge of the literature on monetary and banking problems; not only the Italian (Luigi Einaudi, Achille Loria, Attilio Cabiati, etc.), but also the English and American (Walter Bagehot, Irving Fisher, Hartley Withers, Charles Franklin Dunbar, etc.), and Swedish literature (Gustav Cassel).

The first chapter examines 'The Expansion of Monetary Circulation' (pp.2–17 of the original typescript), during and just after the war, between July 1914 and June 1920. The second chapter, 'Inflation Caused by Banking' (pp.17–26), is concerned with understanding why the mechanisms which had been set up to limit the development of the banks' activities did not operate during these years. The third chapters deals with 'The Effects of Inflation on Prices' (pp.27–31). In chapter 4, Sraffa examines 'The Methods Used in the Past to Return to Sound Money' (pp.31–45), basing his study on Italian and foreign practice. He remarks that:

> the solutions proposed, or applied, for curing an excessive monetary circulation can be reduced to two categories:
> 1 – withdrawal of money from circulation until it has entirely reverted to its original purchasing power;
> 2 – simply refusing to issue new currency while accepting the level of purchasing power actually reached by the currency.[33]

The author discusses both types of solution in the fifth and last chapter, 'The Most Appropriate Remedies for Rehabilitating Italian Circulation in the

Present Situation' (pp.45–64). He believes that the arguments in favour of a return to the pre-war gold standard would be 'more of a moral than of an economic nature'. Such a policy 'would only redress some of the injustices caused by inflation', while having disastrous consequences for production and exchange: this type of deflation necessarily results in a serious economic crisis.[34] Inflation and deflation are not symmetrical as regards their impact on the position of creditors and debtors. Sraffa pronounces himself in favour of the second type of solution, stabilization at the level reached after the war. He concludes his thesis by specifying:

> if we consider that stabilization of exchange rates and stabilization of prices are (in the event of a rise in the value of gold) irreconcilable, it appears to me that the first must be sacrificed in favour of the second, and that it is useful to maintain a circulation of banknotes, despite the serious dangers that might ensue, as long as the future of the price of gold has not been definitively fixed in the most important states of the world.[35]

Sraffa defended his doctoral theses on 29 November 1920 before Einaudi, Gaëtano Mosca (1858–1941), responsible for a 'political class' doctrine which placed him, with Pareto, in the Italian school of the 'élites', and the economist Renzo Fubini.[36] The thesis was received with the highest praise; Einaudi, far from agreeing with all the ideas put forward, thought nevertheless that it was one of the best doctoral theses ever presented at the Law Faculty of Turin. After his thesis, Sraffa familiarized himself with some economic realities by working at a provincial branch bank for a few weeks;[37] he worked in various departments, gaining all-round experience.

After this, he decided to make a study trip to Britain to improve his knowledge, not only of monetary and financial problems, but also of English economic thinking. He was a 'general research student' for three months, from June to August, at the London School of Economics, where, at that time, the climate was rather anti-Marshallian. He attended the lectures given by Theodore Emmanuel Gregory (1893–1971), a specialist in the history of currency and banking[38] who lectured in finance and international economics, and those of Herbert Somerton Foxwell (1849–1936). He was probably more interested and influenced, however, by Edwin Cannan's courses on the theory of value and of distribution; Cannan (1861–1935) was an Adam Smith specialist, who had been teaching at LSE since its foundation in 1895.[39] Meanwhile, Sraffa did not neglect his political and social activities; during his free time he made contacts, and wrote three papers for *L'Ordine Nuovo*.[40]

Sraffa took advantage of his stay in England to get to know John Maynard Keynes, who had just attained international prominence with *The Economic Consequences of the Peace* (1919). How did he manage to make contact with the great economist? The decisive part seems to have been played by a friend of his father, the 'meridionalist' socialist, Gaëtano Salvemini, a professor at the University of Florence, who was a frequent visitor to the house of the famous American art critic, Bernard Berenson. Berenson was a Renaissance specialist and his house, the villa I Tatti, was in Settignano, not far from Florence.[41] As it happened, Keynes had known the Berenson family since 1906.[42] Gaëtano Salvemini recommended the young Italian to the English economist through the good offices of Mary Berenson, the wife of the art critic, who wrote, on 15 June 1921, the following letter of introduction:

> My dear Maynard, this is to introduce to you a great friend of De Salvemini's, a young Signor Sraffa, who is now in London to study English political economy, who of course longs to make your acquaintance. Prof. Salvemini thinks very well of him.[43]

This letter, entrusted to Salvemini, reached Sraffa in London, and was used by him to make the acquaintance of Keynes in Cambridge during August. At the time, Keynes was a regular contributor to the *Manchester Guardian*, where he wrote articles about international monetary problems. From the time of their meeting, the English economist was closely involved in the work and career of the young Italian.

THE ARTICLES ABOUT THE BANK CRISIS IN ITALY AND THE CONFLICT WITH MUSSOLINI

During the academic year 1921–22, Sraffa returned to London to attend another term at LSE, and became increasingly familiar with English classical and neo-classical political economy. He had regular contact with T. E. Gregory, whom he put in touch with his former professor in Turin, Luigi Einaudi.[44]

During this second visit, Sraffa again met Keynes, with whom he discussed monetary issues. Keynes was then editing the weekly supplements dealing with 'reconstruction in Europe', published in four languages by the *Manchester Guardian Commercial*. He asked Sraffa to write on Italian banking problems since the end of the war. This was a great honour, as Keynes had previously only asked prominent individuals, and not just economists, to write for the periodical. In Italy, for example, these included Croce, Francesco-Saverio Nitti and Einaudi. The promised article was ready by spring 1922. Keynes judged the work to be quite exceptional, and decided to publish it, with some corrections, not in the *Manchester Guardian Commercial*, but in the *Economic Journal*, of which he had been the editor since 1912 with the help of Francis Ysidro Edgeworth (1845–1926).

The article came out in June under the title 'The Bank Crisis in Italy'. The study recounts in minute detail the eventful history of the Banca Italiana di

Sconto, from its foundation to its collapse, in December 1921, owing to its links with the Genoese industrial group Ansaldo.[45] Hoping to find solutions to its mounting problems, the group had tried twice, first in 1918 then in 1920 – but without success – to take control of the main Italian bank, the Banca Commerciale Italiana, which the Marsaglia group were also pursuing. Sraffa, who had had access to confidential information, made public some episodes involving the Banca Commerciale Italiana which the Italian press had carefully covered up. He also claimed that the Banca Italiana di Sconto had made large contributions to the Fascist movement. At the end of the article the author addressed the question of the non-application of a law which should have permitted public opinion to control the 'mysterious activities of the financial groups'. He concluded:

> At the time when the factories were occupied by the workers, the Government had solemnly bound itself to get a law passed which would allow the workmen to take part in the control of the industries: once the danger was over, the Bill, as the Minister of Labour himself said, was put to sleep. And now new laws are demanded to prevent the formation of trusts, to protect the independence of banks, to regulate the reserves to be held on banking deposits, notwithstanding that the experience of other countries has proved the impossibility of remedying such evils by legislative reforms. But even if these laws were not futile in themselves, what could be their use as long as the Government is prepared to be the first to break them so soon as it is blackmailed by a band of gunmen or a group of bold financiers?[46]

The article, which ends on a very open and direct note, nevertheless went completely unnoticed in the Italian press. We will see later that, in contrast, a second article on the same subject produced an immediate reaction at the highest level.

In June 1922, Sraffa returned to his native country to stay with his parents in Milan (1 via Ugo Foscolo). Not long afterwards, he was given a job with the socialist city council of Milan: he was to set up and direct an office for the collection of labour statistics.[47] He did not stay in the job very long: political events were moving much faster and, on 30 October, the Fascist government came into power. As a gesture of protest, Sraffa decided to resign his job with the city council.

It was at about that time that Keynes asked him whether he could write another article about the bank crisis in Italy, which would this time be published in the supplements of the *Manchester Guardian Commercial*. The article, 'Italian Banking Today', was published on 7 December 1922.[48] In it, Sraffa examines the consequences of the collapse of the Banca di Sconto on the Italian banking system, while explaining the devices used by the major banks when presenting their formal accounts. He criticized the Consorzio per Sovvenzioni su Valori Industriali, an institution which had been created during the war, and which was supposed to tidy up the situation. Although the paper was not mentioned in the Italian press, it aroused the anger, both of the head of the government, Benito Mussolini, and of the management of the Banca Commerciale Italiana. On 20 December 1922, Mussolini sent a first telegram to Rector Angelo Sraffa, describing the paper as 'an act of pure and simple banking defeatism, and an act of true and real sabotage to Italian finance'. He added that 'his being a socialist does not entitle him to spread abroad mistrust in the institutions of Italian finance – I give warning that I reserve my right to demand by other means a very strict account of this scurvy act'.[49] The following day, 21 December, Mussolini sent a second telegram to the Rector requiring him to ask his son for an immediate retraction.[50] Angelo Sraffa responded with a courageous letter to the Duce, wherein he explained that his son's article had only stated known facts which had never been denied, and that it did not, therefore, need a retraction.

Piero Sraffa took refuge for a few days in Lugano, in Switzerland. For his part, the managing director of the Banca Commerciale Italiana, Giuseppe Toeplitz, summoned Piero Sraffa, who took a solicitor with him to attend the meeting. The bank did not, however, succeed in initiating legal proceedings against him. Still, this episode led Sraffa to curtail his militant activities. When, later, he reminisced about that period to Luca Meldolesi, he said:

> I had to cut off all contact with the Italian Communists.... Obviously, my parents were very pleased...[51]

Keynes, who may have felt in some degree responsible for the troubles his young friend found himself in, decided on 9 January 1923, to invite him to stay again in Britain. Sraffa accepted, and had no difficulty in obtaining a passport on 20 January, and, two days later, a visa from the English consulate in Milan. However, on landing at Dover on 26 January, he had an unpleasant surprise. He was questioned for three hours by the police, then, following an order by the Secretary of State, he was sent back to Calais as an undesirable alien, in implementation of an article of the Aliens Act.[52] Sraffa went to Paris, where he attempted to take some action on the matter. The ban on entering English territory probably stemmed from a request by Mussolini's Ministry of Foreign Affairs. Keynes applied to John Colin Campbell Davidson, who was the Prime Minister's Parliamentary Private Secretary, mentioning that the article which had aroused the anger of the head of the Italian government was 'a harmless and rather dull article but a little more candid in its criticism of some of the banks than is usual'.[53] He added that 'it surely cannot be the business of our Home Office to abet the more outrageous stupidity of Mussolini'.[54] His intervention proved fruitless, and Sraffa was unable to enter

Britain before the latter half of 1924, after Keynes, following the advent of the first Labour government, had finally managed to get Sraffa's name struck off the list of undesirable aliens .

SOME IMPORTANT RELATIONSHIPS: GOBETTI, MATTIOLI, ROSSELLI

Despite his troubles with the new Fascist regime, Sraffa decided to embark on a university career in Italy. In November 1923, he was appointed a lecturer at the Faculty of Law in Perugia, where he taught political economy and, in 1925–6, public finance as well. Although his stance was opposed theoretically to the dominant marginal approach, he did not seem in his lectures to put forward any direct criticisms of the Italian representatives of this school, such as Maffeo Pantaleoni, the author of the famous *Principii di economia pura* (1889) and Vilfredo Pareto, who published, after settling in Lausanne, the *Cours d'économie politique* (1896–97), then the *Manuale di economia politica* (1906). His criticisms were rather directed against Marshall's theory of value and distribution, and this was to lead to his seminal article of 1925.[55]

From 1923 onwards, Sraffa became friendly with a number of young intellectuals, and some of these relationships were to prove very long lasting. In Turin, to begin with, he made contact, during 1923, with Piero Gobetti (1901–26), a former student of his father's at the Faculty of Law, and also a student of Umberto Cosmo's. Reconciling liberalism with socialism, but also a fervent anti-fascist, the young Gobetti had been involved with the first series of Gramsci's *L'Ordine Nuovo*; in 1922, he launched a weekly paper, *La Rivoluzione Liberale: Rivista storica settimanale di politica.* Sraffa did not wish to be a member of the editorial committee of this journal, which was to be banned in 1924. He seems nevertheless to have agreed to publish, in October 1923, a highly satirical article, 'Opinioni', which took as its target a Fascist note 'La lira italiana continua a migliorare', published in Mussolini's newspaper, *Il Popolo d'Italia*, on 10 October 1923, concerning the fluctuations of the lira on the exchange market. After reproducing the whole of this note, he makes the following commentary:

> Let us try to find our bearings. The *Italian lira* 'has lost slightly in relation to France' although 'the French franc has lost ground in relation to the other four countries' (including Italy). The lira 'has gone up in relation to three other countries' (Switzerland, the United States, Great Britain), but it is not known how much Switzerland and Great Britain have gained against Italy. Conclusion: 'an improvement of the Italian lira'. The *French franc* 'loses in relation to the other four countries', but three lines later, it

finds the means to recover; it gains against Italy and stays on a par with sterling. 'Thus, absolute depreciation of the French franc.' *Sterling* 'has remained stable in relation to France' (which 'has lost ground in relation to all the others', including sterling); it has 'risen in relation to the United States and Italy' (while Italy and the United States, by chance, prevailed over the lira). 'Relative degradation of sterling'. The *dollar*. No, this is enough; let the reader continue the analysis, provided he is still alive. But at his own expense. As far as we are concerned, we deem it right to recognize the intense patriotic feeling which has moved the intelligent compiler of the Fascist financial note; it certainly aims at persuading international banking circles of the opportunity to speculate on the rise of the Italian Lira, and we do not have the slightest doubt as to the success which will follow this initiative.[56]

In Milan, Sraffa got to know two important young academics, Raffaele Mattioli and Carlo Rosselli.

When the First World War started, Raffaele Mattioli (1895–1973) was an 'interventionist', and volunteered when Italy entered the conflict in 1915. At the end of the war, he followed Gabriele D'Annunzio on his expedition to Fiume. After a liberalistic education at the Commercial High School in Genoa, he prepared, under the supervision of Attilio Cabiati, a doctoral thesis in economics on the brand new proposals of Irving Fisher that were supposed to secure the 'stabilization' of the currency, 'Note storico-critiche intorno al progetto Fisher per la "stabilizzazione" della moneta'. This thesis was defended in December 1920.[57] The following year, he was assistant in economics under Attilio Cabiati and Luigi Einaudi at the Bocconi University in Milan. The Rector, Angelo Sraffa, asked him to take charge of the library. In addition, he was editor in chief of the *Rivista Bancaria*[58] from 1920 to 1922. From 1922 to 1925, he was General Secretary of the Milan Chamber of Commerce. The managing director of the Banca Commerciale Italiana, Giuseppe Toeplitz, persuaded him to join the bank in 1925 as head of his secretarial staff. This gave Mattioli access to a great deal of confidential economic information about the Fascist regime, and he enabled his friend Sraffa to make good use of this. Sraffa, in turn, shared information with Antonio Gramsci, and then, later, with friends such as Angelo Tasca and Giorgio Amendola.

From December 1923 onwards, Sraffa was in contact with a cousin of his from the Treves family, Carlo Rosselli (1899–1937), who had just obtained a job as an unpaid assistant in economics to Einaudi for 1923–4 at the Bocconi University.[59] The Rector soon developed a high opinion of him, and suggested that he collaborate on the review he was about to start up for the Institute of Political Economy, the *Annali di Economia*.[60] Carlo Rosselli and

Sraffa launched into lively discussions not only about economic matters, but also about politics. A nephew of Claudio Treves (1869–1933) – a reformist socialist leader close to Filippo Turati – Rosselli defended two doctoral theses: first, 'Il sindacalismo', in Florence in 1921, and then, 'Prime linee di una teoria economica dei sindicati operai', in Sienna in 1923. During the summer of 1923, he took part in a seminar organized in Britain by the Fabian Society, from which he came back highly impressed by the writings of Sidney and Beatrice Webb, and by those of George Douglas Howard Cole, exponent of 'Guild Socialism'.

Rosselli was a non–Marxist socialist whose sympathies went to the Partito Socialista Unitario, born of a split within the Italian Socialist Party after the congress of October 1922, and led by Filippo Turati and Giacomo Matteotti (1885–1925). He contributed to the theoretical journal *La Critica Sociale.* In the spring of 1924, he intended to create a laboratory of socio-economic studies which was to establish the basis for a Fabian Society in Italy, and asked Sraffa to join him and two intellectuals close to the Unitary Socialist Party: Nino Levi, assistant at the Bocconi University, and Alessandro Schiavi. Filippo Turati and his companion Anna Kuliscioff were very much in favour of this initiative, which would, according to them, be extremely useful for the future of the party.[61] The idea materialized a little while later in a small institute of social studies named after Giacomo Matteotti, an opposition leader assassinated by the Fascists on 12 June 1924. The president was Turati and the secretary Alessandro Schiavi.[62] It was to be very short-lived, and there is no clear evidence that Sraffa had any real participation in its deliberations. The promise he had made to them has nevertheless given credence, mistakenly, to the idea that he was politically close to the Unitary Socialist Party.[63]

CRITICAL POSITIONS IN ECONOMIC THEORY AND SUCCESS IN THE COMPETITION OF THE UNIVERSITY OF CAGLIARI

In October 1924, Sraffa was again able to go to Britain without the risk of being refused entry. He lived in London and, later, in Cambridge.[64] He saw Keynes during that trip and, at the end of November, Keynes asked him to write a short article for the *Economic Journal* about the work of Maffeo Pantaleoni, the father of Italian marginal analysis, who had just died. Why did he ask Sraffa? Because Achille Loria, official correspondent of the Royal Economic Society, had just sent an obituary to the editorial office of the journal, and Keynes thought it much too short and superficial. In his article, which was published in December 1924,[65] Sraffa provided biographical details about the 'prince' of Italian economists, who had sided with the Fascists. He related his career as a 'Don Quixote of Italian politics'; he emphasized his moral qualities and his role as a denouncer of banking scandals, and described Pantaleoni's monograph *La Caduta del Credito Mobiliare* as a 'veritable masterpiece'. The *Principii di economia pura* (1889) 'was the first organic treatise in which – in accordance with the teachings of Marshall – the doctrines of the classical writers were harmonized with the new theories of Gossen and Jevons', and, at the same time, 'the most efficacious disseminator of the theory of utility in Italy as well as in other Latin countries'.[66] Influenced by Richard Jennings, Hermann Heinrich Gossen, Williams S. Jevons and Alfred Marshall,[67] but also by Carl Menger, *Pure Economics* formed a bridge between the English neo-classical school and the Austrian one, in spite of the fact that Pantaleoni denied the innovative character of the latter. Pantaleoni merged the classical theory of cost with the theory of marginal utility, with quite different results from those reached by Alfred Marshall in his *Principles of Economics* (1890).

During the second half of 1924, the young Sraffa translated the book Keynes had published the previous year, *A Tract on Monetary Reform*, into Italian. His translation was published in Milan, in January 1925.[68] The same year he was approached by the editor of the *Giornale degli Economisti*[69] to review several books. He prepared a review of a book by an American supporter of the theory of crises based on under-consumption, H. B. Hastings: *Costs and Profits, their Relation to Business Cycles*.[70] In 1926, he published two reviews, one of a small handbook on currency, the other of a doctoral thesis devoted to the Italian banking system between 1912 and 1922.[71] The following year, he published a note about a book by an English exchange broker, H. W. Phillips, *Modern Foreign Exchange and Foreign Banking*.[72]

Between 1924 and spring 1925, Sraffa worked on a major essay that attacked the foundations of the orthodox analysis of the great English neo-classical theorist, Alfred Marshall:[73] 'Sulle relazioni fra costo e quantità prodotta'. The essay came out in November 1925 in the *Annali di Economia* of the Bocconi University.[74] Sraffa examined the law of non-proportional returns in Marshall's model of static partial equilibrium, which established a symmetry between relations of demand and supply as regards the value of commodities. Previously, classical economists had given prominence to two separate laws of returns. The law of *increasing* returns was created by Adam Smith and associated with the process of the division of labour in industry – a problem of dynamics, in the category of 'production'. The law of *diminishing* returns, on the contrary, set forth by Turgot, then by David Ricardo in connection with the problem of agricultural rent, is also a problem of dynamics, but in the category of 'distribution'. Marshall tried to combine these two orientations in a single law of non-proportional returns, to set up his theory of prices. This law can be represented by a U-shaped curve, connecting average cost and output. The situation of a firm is studied, independently of that of other firms, in a framework of free competition. In this model, the normal case is that of diminishing returns (or increasing costs).

Sraffa foregrounded how Marshall's explanation concerning the exceptional existence of increasing returns (diminishing costs) evolved '*internal* economies' followed by '*external* economies' of the firm. He nevertheless developed his attack to focus criticism on the problem of diminishing returns. In Marshall's theory, the supply curve of a firm is independent of the supply curve of other firms and moving from the firm to the industry, the aggregate means a simple transposition. According to Sraffa, this analysis is unacceptable, because it does not take the interdependences into account: the conditions of production of a firm necessarily have an effect on those of its competitors. After having shown the incompatibility between the case of diminishing returns and the conditions of particular equilibrium, Sraffa concludes by considering, for the particular industry, 'the case of constant costs as being normal, rather than that of increasing or diminishing costs', in keeping with the opinion of Ricardo. This situation is, to his mind, the only one compatible with the equilibrium of free competition, or at least a 'first approximation of reality'.

There are numerous footnotes in the article that indicate the author's extensive knowledge of the literature. Besides references to Turgot, to the classical economists, to the Italian marginalists (Enrico Barone, Umberto Ricci, etc.), one finds references to many English-speaking writers: Charles J. Bullock, John Harold Clapham, Francis Ysidro Edgeworth, Alfred William Flux, Arthur Cecil Pigou, Philip Wicksteed, but also John Elliot Cairnes, John Neville Keynes and Henry Sigwick; there is even a reference to Arthur Lyon Bowley's *Mathematical Groundwork of Economics*. There are also references to *The Industrial System* (1909) by J. A. Hobson and to *The Distribution of Wealth* (1893) by the institutionalist John R. Commons.

Sraffa was unquestionably interested in classical political economy, but what about Marx's critique of political economy? It is not easy today to determine precisely what might have been Sraffa's opinion of Marx's *Capital* during 1924–25. He certainly discussed the book with Gramsci, with Mattioli, with Rosselli, and maybe even with Antonio Graziadei (1873–1953), a friend of his father. Graziadei, a professor of Parma University and an important member of the Italian Socialist Party, engaged, during the years 1895–1900, in a systematic critique of the Marxist theory of value, while defending the 'theory of surplus labour' combining it with a new theory of profit. He joined the Italian Communist Party at its foundation, and was the head of its right wing; at the same time, he completed his previous criticisms of the Marxist theory of value. His book, *Prezzo e sovraprezzo nell' economia capitalistica*, published in 1923, was condemned in July 1924 by George Zinoviev from the platform of the Fifth Congress of the Communist International; also condemned were *Marxism and Philosophy* by Karl Korsch and *History and Class Consciousness* by Georg Lukács.[75] Sraffa was well acquainted with the works of Graziadei concerning Marx, which, moreover, were sent to him by the author at regular intervals, but he did not appear to be convinced by their content, and in any case did not want to be drawn into a discussion about the theses expressed therein. In a letter of 13 February 1925, he wrote 'Thank you for your new work which I received in Perugia and which I have read with great interest', without giving any further details. He announced that, in exchange, he was sending his translation of Keynes's essay, A *Tract on Monetary Reform.* Giorgio Gattei, who published the letter, indicates that Graziadei's book must have been either *Il prezzo e il sovraprezzo in rapporto ai consumatori e ai lavoratori* or *La concezione del sopralavoro e la teoria del valore*, both published in Rome.[76]

In the middle of the decade, Sraffa intended to continue with his academic career. He applied to the University of Cagliari, in Sardinia, where a competition had been organized for three chairs at the end of 1925. The competition commission was under the presidency of Augusto Graziani (1865–1944), an eclectic economist who attempted to reconcile historicism and marginalism. The other members were Constantino Bresciani-Turroni (1882–1963), Attilio Cabiati (1872–1950), Lorenzo Mossa (1886–1957), the secretary of the commission, the only jurist, Professor of Commercial Law at Cagliari, former student of Angelo Sraffa, and Umberto Ricci (1879–1949), the reporter of the commission. With the exception of Mossa,[77] they were all opponents of Fascism. The commission sat from 5 to 9 January 1926. There were eleven candidates, but only six applications were considered, those of Carlo Grilli, Angelo Fraccacreta, Roberto Michels, Giuseppe-Ugo Papi, Carlo Rosselli and Sraffa. The commission immediately rejected the candidature of Roberto Michels (1876–1936) because it thought his work to be outside the field of economics and more closely related to sociology and political science. It also rejected, though not without some praise, Rosselli, who was thought not to have produced sufficient theoretical work, and Papi because his thinking was still confused and contradictory, although he had a good aptitude for research.[78] Three candidates were finally accepted; they each received five votes: Carlo Grilli, responsible for statistics at the Ministry of Public Works,[79] Sraffa, and Angelo Fraccacreta, a lecturer at the University of Naples, and, later, at the University of Messina.[80]

The comments of the commission are particularly instructive:

> The scholarly output of this candidate is not very plentiful: it is limited to a memoir on 'Relationships between cost and quantity produced', a memoir on 'Monetary inflation in Italy during and after the war', an article published in the *Economic Journal* about the bank crisis in Italy (dealing

> with the fall of the Banca di Sconto), an obituary of Pantaleoni, and a note on 'The situation of Italian banks' in the commercial supplement of *The Manchester Guardian.* The commission particularly praised the first of these works, in which the author confronts one of the most difficult themes in pure economics; it nevertheless criticized the conclusion which the author had reached. It also noted the obvious concern of the author to appear succinct and concise, which has at times led him to complex constructions and to a sobriety verging on obscurity. But it cannot be denied that the author is already asserting himself as a rigorous thinker and a level-headed critical mind, and that he has a comprehensive knowledge of the literature of his subject.
>
> The essay on the bank crisis as well as the very brief but salty *Manchester Guardian* note also confirm the author's skill in his observation and judicious interpretation of economic facts. The commission thus unanimously recognizes that the candidate is mature enough to teach in a university.[81]

Right till the end of his career, when he published *Production of Commodities by Means of Commodities,* Sraffa was always to be characterized by the very limited quantity of his academic output, linked to an extreme conciseness. It should be noted that the competition commission rejected, without any precise justification, the conclusion of the article of 1925, and mentioned with some humour the 'salty note' in the *Manchester Guardian*, which had provoked the wrath of Benito Mussolini.

On 1 March 1926, Sraffa got a professorship in economics at the age of twenty-eight. He was to teach in the capital of Sardinia until the summer of 1927.

The 1925 article, largely ignored by Italian economists, was very well received in Britain, particularly by Edgeworth, who advised Keynes to ask the young economist to write a shorter paper on the same subject for the *Economic Journal.* In his letter of acceptance, addressed to Keynes on 6 June 1926, Sraffa, very pleased to have interested Edgeworth, summarized the theoretical position of the essay, and sketched out roughly the path he intended to explore. In particular, he mentioned that:

> It is generally supposed that two theories for the extreme cases, perfect competition and perfect monopoly, are sufficient; reality must be somewhere between. I think it can be proved that so soon as any imperfection is introduced in a system of competition (and such an imperfection in general takes the form of some sort of differentiation between the products of different producers of the same commodity) equilibrium is reached in a way extremely similar to that of monopoly and very far from that of competition.[82]

The promised essay came out in the *Economic Journal*, in December 1926, under the title 'The Laws of Returns under Competitive Conditions'.[83] As will be seen later, it was to have, during the following years, a profound impact on some of the most gifted of the young Cambridge economists. The author summed up the main points of his 1925 article, and declared that the theoretical perspective of free competition should be abandoned in favour of monopoly. For him, 'everyday experience shows that a very large number of undertakings – and the majority of those which produce manufactured consumers' goods – work under conditions of diminishing individual costs'.[84]

Sraffa also glimpsed a new perspective for neo-classical economic theory: 'imperfect competition'. Yet he did not himself appear to be really convinced of the fruitfulness of that approach, since he rejected the whole Marshallian theory.[85] In this study, he observed that the theory of value, as represented by the well-known Marshallian metaphor of the scissors of demand and supply, no longer aroused controversy, as it had in the nineteenth century, but was the subject of a consensus among economists. In respect of this, he noted:

> Sceptics might perhaps think that the agreement in question is due, not so much to everyone being convinced, as to the indifference felt by the majority nowadays in regard to the theory of value – an indifference which is justified by the fact that this theory, more than any other part of economic theory, has lost much of its direct bearing upon practical politics, and particularly in regard to doctrines of social changes, which had formerly been conferred upon it by Ricardo and afterwards by Marx, and in opposition to them by the bourgeois economists.[86]

THE DECISION TO EMIGRATE TO BRITAIN

Around the middle of the twenties, the Fascist regime greatly stepped up the repression of political opponents. On 30 December 1925, the Council of Ministers, under Mussolini's presidency, decided to adopt 'all necessary means to safeguard the moral and material interests of the nation'; all the opposition newspapers were immediately seized, and during the following weeks, the anti-fascist groups were disbanded. In 1926, Rosselli – who, with Gaëtano Salvemini, was one of the founding members of the first anti-fascist underground newspaper, *Non Mollare!*[87] – was forbidden to teach in Genoa. Salvemini sought refuge in London, and took up a career as an anti-fascist lecturer on the university circuit. The political situation worsened brutally toward the end of 1926. A mysterious failed attempt on Mussolini's life, attributed to Anteo Zamboni, on 31 October, was used as a pretext to set up 'laws for the defence of the State'. Preparations for the 'leggi fascistissime' had been made by the Minister of Justice, Alfredo Rocco. They stipulated:

– cancellation of all passports and severe repression of clandestine emigration;

– disbanding of all anti-fascist parties and newspapers;

– creation of banishment and confinement (*confino*) for opponents of the regime.

Two institutions were to apply this new legislation: a political police force, the Vigilance and Repression of Anti-fascists Organization (VRAO) and the Special Court for the Defence of the State.

From that date, many of Sraffa's friends were wanted by the police. Rosselli, who, with Pietro Nenni, edited the weekly *Il Quarto Stato*, in Milan, from March to October 1926, was arrested in December for having organized Turati's escape to France; he was sentenced to five years' confinement on the island of Lipari. On 8 November, Gramsci was arrested and sentenced to five years' confinement on the island of Ustica, near Palermo. At the end of 1926, Sraffa feared that the Fascist regime would do the same to him. At any rate, the anti-fascist teachers had to prepare themselves for a hard time. At the beginning of January 1927, Sraffa tried to obtain a chair at the University of Genoa, where he would have been closer to the Milan family home – apparently without success. But at the end of January, an extraordinary opportunity to emigrate was presented to him. On 25 January 1927, Keynes wrote to Sraffa:

> Your article in the December *Journal* has been very much liked over here. Everyone I have spoken to agrees that it puts you in the front rank of the younger economists. Pigou is extremely interested, and has been looking up your Italian article. You may be interested to know that he feels he must, in the light of it, reconsider his whole position.

He then disclosed that the University of Cambridge would be ready to offer him a lectureship, created specially for him, of indefinite duration.[88] Although his command of English was not very good at that time, Sraffa accepted this offer with joy, giving his answer on 6 February. On 30 May, the Appointments Committee of Cambridge elected him to a lectureship in economics at King's College to take effect from 1 October 1927, for four years in the first instance.[89]

At the beginning of September, Sraffa arrived in London, where he stayed for a while before moving on to Cambridge. But before describing his new life there, it will be necessary to study his remarkable relationship with Gramsci, and his role as the intermediary between the imprisoned philosopher and the Italian Communist Party.

2 Affinities with communism: a notable friendship with Antonio Gramsci

JOURNALIST AT *L'ORDINE NUOVO*

Piero Sraffa's political position became more radical after 1917, although he never was a member of the Italian Communist Party[1] and always maintained an independent position in relation to it. On his return from the war in 1919–20, he joined the team of *L'Ordine Nuovo*, which was edited by Gramsci, and continued contributing even after the journal had become the first daily of the new party in 1921–22. During his first trip to Britain, in the summer of 1921, he carried a press card from *L'Ordine Nuovo*, and in London he contacted the editors of *The Labour Monthly: A Magazine of International Labour*. This Marxist magazine, which first appeared in July 1921, had been launched by a communist of Indian origin, (Rajani) Palme Dutt. The magazine contained theoretical analyses and gave information about the class struggle in the main capitalist countries. Sraffa agreed to be its Italian correspondent. While in London, he also sent three articles to his friends in Turin; they were immediately published in *L'Ordine Nuovo*.

The first article, 'Open Shop Drive', subtitled 'Come la classe borghese americana combatte l'organizzazione operaia – Boicottaggio e spionaggio – Come si spezza uno sciopero – Il "cane giallo"',[2] was signed P. S. It dealt with labour struggles in the United States, using as its source an anthology of texts recently published in New York about the 'open shop' system which had been set up by manufacturers and was, in theory, meant to ensure that non-members of trade unions could also be employed, but was in fact used to exclude trade union members, as was shown by numerous examples.[3] The second article, 'Industriali e governo inglese contro i lavoratori', unsigned, dealt with the labour movement in Britain. According to Sraffa, the government and the manufacturers were attacking the labour movement with the specific aim of 'restoring the absolute authority of the employer'. Sraffa supported this with an account of the abolition of numerous joint commissions which had been created to arbitrate conflicts. He concluded with the assertion that:

> The English working class has been unable to free itself from illusions of a possible reconciliation between capital and labour, and of the impartiality of the Government: the industrialists' blinkered reaction, in actual fact, is helping to raise the consciousness of the proletariat.[4]

The third article, 'I "Labour Leaders"', identifying its author as 'Nostra corrispondenza particolare (P.S.)', elaborated more on political and social notions. The author severely criticized the attitude of trade union leaders who, in 1921, were being challenged by their own members. Sraffa phrased his criticism in the following terms:

> There is not very much difference between English labour leaders and the trade union bureaucrats on the continent. They are petty bourgeois and closely bound to the capitalist system; they are ready to 'improve' this system, that is to say, to modify the balance of forces in such a way as to increase their influence. In the hierarchy of social classes, they are just below the grande bourgeoisie and hope one day to be able to overtake it: they are thus in favour of all the reforms that might weaken it, from wealth tax to nationalization of mines and railways. In order to reach their objective, they speculate on the strength of the proletariat and try to blackmail the grande bourgeoisie by showing it glimpses of the spectre of revolution: but as soon as this spectre threatens to take shape, they immediately become frightened and unite with the bourgeoisie to fight it. They are petty bourgeois and do not want to jeopardize the whole structure of which they are co-owners .... And in England, the moderation, the opportunism and the corporatism of the leaders correspond to the feelings of the majority of workers. Between the leadership and the masses, the actual difference – and it is all to the advantage of the masses – is only a difference in degree, but the watchword is the same. Or more precisely the absence of a watchword, of a common objective towards which everyone would strive, an organic programme from which a real solution could be drawn, a solution specific to each problem as it comes up; in fact this is the void which is hiding behind an apolitical stance .... In substance, this apolitical stance consists in stopping the working class from exercising, as a class, an influence on the general policy of the State.
>
> As the proletariat is entirely lacking in political preparation and organization, its action is necessarily limited to the industrial domain, and its leaders do all they can to confine it to that. But goodwill is not sufficient to remedy the theoretical and practical absurdity of separating the economic struggle from the political struggle.[5]

Back in Italy, Sraffa decided to give up his post as a correspondent for the *Labour Monthly* because he felt he was insufficiently informed about Italian social problems. He asked Gramsci if he knew of someone else who would be more suitable for the position. Gramsci advised him to contact Andrea Viglongo (1900–86), who, in 1919, was already one of the principal journalists of *L'Ordine Nuovo*; Viglongo could write the articles and Sraffa would translate them into English. But the suggestion came to nothing.[6]

A SERIOUS CONTROVERSY WITH GRAMSCI ABOUT THE MEANS OF FIGHTING FASCISM

After his second return to Italy, in June 1922, Sraffa seems to have had less contact than before with his friends at *L'Ordine Nuovo*. Gramsci had gone to Moscow at the end of May 1922 as the delegate of the Italian Communist Party to the Executive Committee of the Third International.[7] The Italian Communist Party, under the direction of Amadeo Bordiga, had been openly opposed to the International's line of action since the resolutions of the Third Congress (July 1921), and to the theses of the Executive Committee of December 1921, relating to the 'united front' policy. During the second half of 1923, Gramsci set up a new party leadership, which was to apply the International's line of action. He left Moscow at the beginning of December and settled in Vienna, where he organized, at the request of the Executive Committee, an 'External Bureau' of the Italian Communist Party. He tried to renew contact with the intellectuals who had participated in *L'Ordine Nuovo*, including Sraffa. He asked his friend to contribute to a Marxist review which he was planning to launch, *Critica Proletaria*, but which did not, in fact, come into being.

Sraffa accepted, and they exchanged letters about the Italian political situation and the problem of organizing the struggle against Fascism. In a letter of February or March 1924, Sraffa explained:

> I maintain my opinion that the working class is entirely absent from political life; and I can only conclude that the Communist Party can, *today*, achieve nothing positive, or almost nothing. The situation is strangely similar to that of 1916–17; and the same can be said of my feelings, which you say are similar to those of other friends who have written to you. My political opinions have not changed – worse, they have hardened .... There will be no possibility of political action by the working class for as long as the problems facing individual workers have to be solved individually and privately, as is the case today; they have to rely on themselves to protect their jobs, wages, houses and families; the union and the party cannot be of any help, on the contrary ... .

He added:

> The urgent problem, arising before any other, is that of 'liberty' and 'order': the others will come up later, but they cannot for the moment interest the workers. I do not believe that the Communist Party can today lessen Fascist pressure: it is the time for democratic opposition movements and I feel we should let them act and even help them along. Before anything else, we need a 'bourgeois revolution', and only then will labour politics be able to develop.

As for the parties of the left, he thinks that it is:

> a mistake to oppose them openly and to pour too much scorn on bourgeois 'liberty' (as is done, for example, by *L'Unità*): whether it is thought to be beautiful or ugly, this is what the workers need most at the moment and it is an indispensable condition of all further conquests .... The Communist Party could only campaign for freedom and against dictatorship in general by contradicting itself: yet it makes a terrible mistake when it gives the impression it is sabotaging an alliance of opposition movements .... You say correctly that Fascism is at the moment breaking up the unity of the State and that today's problem is urgent, but I do not believe that the problem is of the kind you mention; it seems to me to be more a problem of class and not of the police ... .[8]

Here Sraffa was giving his friend a real political 'lecture', and Gramsci, although he was irritated by some of these remarks, thought that it would be valuable to have them discussed by the militants of the party. He had extracts from the letter, together with his own reply, published under the title 'Problems of Today and Tomorrow' in *L'Ordine Nuovo*, which could again be published legally in Italy in March 1924, but only for a short period. Gramsci vigorously challenged Sraffa, but at the same time attempted to spare his friend's feelings:

> In this letter are contained all the elements necessary and sufficient for the liquidation of such a revolutionary organization as our party is and should be. This, however, is not the intention of our friend S., who, although he has never joined our ranks, and although he lives on the fringes of our movement and propaganda, has faith in our party and considers it to be the only one capable of solving in a lasting way the problems posed and the situation created by Fascism... S. believes that the future belongs to our party. But how can it continue to exist, how can the Communist Party continue to develop, how can it hope to be in a position, after the fall of Fascism, to dominate and guide events, if it destroys itself in an absolute passivity such as that suggested by this same S.?

Further on, he notes that:

> Our friend S. has so far not been able to rid himself of all the ideological residues of his democratic-liberal intellectual background, that is to say, normative and Kantian, non–Marxist and non-dialectical. What meaning can be attached to the statements he makes, to the effect that the working class is 'absent', that the situation is unfavourable to the trade union and the Party, that fascist violence is a problem of 'order', that is, of 'police', and not of 'class'? ... Systematic, legal repression is today pressing upon the proletariat; on the other hand there has been a slackening round the edges of this repression, as it has been directed against those strata which, in 1920, were its allies only from the objective standpoint, and which are reorganizing, and partly re-entering the fray, through their acceptance of a watered-down image of constitutional opposition, i. e. their most overtly petty bourgeois character ... . The working class is, and will remain, 'absent' for as long as the Communist Party allows constitutional opposition to monopolize the awakening of the struggle of the social classes which are historically the allies of the proletariat. The birth and strengthening of constitutional opposition movements bring new strength to the proletariat, which is again flocking to the Party and the trade unions. If the Communist Party intervenes actively in the process of shaping the various opposition movements, it is trying to achieve a class differentiation in the social base of the opposition, getting the peasant masses to move towards a programme of peasant and worker government, and we can now see that the proletariat is no longer 'absent' as it was before. We see a line of political action where today's problems are solved, as well as those of tomorrow, and where the future is being prepared and organized, and is not simply a result of fate. This line of political action is thus contrary, not only to constitutional opposition, but also to Fascism .... The truth is that constitutional opposition will never carry through its programme, that it is nothing but an instrument of agitation against Fascism ... .[9]

In turn, Gramsci had given his economist friend a sharp political 'lecture'.

At about the same time, he sent to his comrades at the head of the Italian Communist Party a letter containing some particularly interesting details about his appreciation of Sraffa's position:

> Sraffa is now moving towards a position which seems to me to be very much that of a Maximalist ... .[10] Sraffa is going to collaborate in the *Rassegna*,[11] and I can quite believe, in view of what he has written to me, that his contribution will be very interesting – as far as he is concerned, the problem does not appear very complex; he has remained isolated since

> the contact he had with us in Turin, and his activities never brought him into contact with workers, but he is certainly still a Marxist, and keeping in touch with him will be enough to straighten him out and make him an active element of our Party, to which he will be useful in many ways, now as well as later.
>
> There is, in his letter, a passage which is not to be published, but which is very interesting: about the trade union problem, he asks me why our party never thought of creating trade unions similar to the American IWW [Industrial Workers of the World], which was perfectly adapted to the situation of illegality, and to the violent repression exercised by the State and the private organisms of capitalism. He has promised to send me an article about trade union bureaucracy in which he will, I believe, also develop this theme, which appears to me to be very important. It is true that we have never asked ourselves, in practical terms, the question of the possible creation of an underground, centralized trade union movement, which would work towards creating a new state of affairs among the working class. Our groups, as well as our Trade Union Committee, have, inside the Confederazione Generale del Lavoro, retained their characteristics as a party, and as a party fraction; this is necessary, but does not solve the whole problem. Neither would it be possible to solve it by following the model of the IWW, which was, in practice, the organization of workers known as 'migrants'; nevertheless, the way the IWW had been organized might give us some further information and might help to define the nature of the problem.[12]

It seems that Sraffa never wrote the article about trade union bureaucracy that he had promised for *L'Ordine Nuovo*, which continued to come out regularly up to April 1925. Gramsci returned to Italy in May 1924, after a two-year absence; he was elected to parliament, and, in August, became General Secretary of the Italian Communist Party; it was then that he began the struggle against the supporters of Amadeo Bordiga.

He was again able to meet his friend. There is unfortunately no precise record of the subjects they discussed during the period 1924–6. They certainly debated the economic and political climate of Fascist Italy. Sraffa advised the Communist leader to read the *Prospettive economiche*: a collective of syntheses, accompanied by a forecast of the performance of the Italian economy, which Giorgio Mortara had been working on at the Bocconi University since 1921.[13] He shared with his friend the confidential economic information he was getting from Mattioli, who had been working since 1925 on the secretarial staff of the managing director of the Banca Commerciale Italiana. So it was most probably Sraffa who gave the economic data which ended up in the report commissioned by the leadership of the Italian Communist Party, 'Un esame della situazione Italiana' (2–3 August 1926).[14] Gramsci was interested in Sraffa's theoretical work on competition; he kept chiding him for writing so little, for hesitating to develop his ideas in articles. Sraffa's comment about this was that:

> In the past, Nino [Antonio Gramsci] always chided me for having too many scientific scruples, saying that this stopped me from writing anything: I have never been cured of that illness ... .[15]

It does not appear that the Communist leader advised Sraffa to consider particular themes for his research, such as the theory of value, for example, or that he encouraged him to set aside monetary or banking problems in order to concentrate on Ricardo's theory. They probably discussed Ricardo, and certainly Marx, but there is no written trace of this.

MATERIAL AND MORAL SUPPORT FOR THE IMPRISONED COMMUNIST LEADER, AND ORGANIZATION OF HIS DEFENCE

On 8 November 1926, in Rome, the Fascist police arrested Gramsci at the same time as the other main leaders of the Communist Party; initially the prisoner was sentenced to five years' confinement on the island of Ustica, off the coast of Palermo. For the next eleven years, Sraffa put all his strength into helping his friend. Being temporarily allowed to read and write, Gramsci immediately wrote to Sraffa to obtain books and reviews of general interest; he specially wanted a 'sound treatise on economics and finance', so as to study the subject.[16] Sraffa bought some books, opened an unlimited account for the prisoner at the Milan bookshop of Sperling and Kupfer, and told him that he was ready to help him financially.[17] Among the books on economics sent to Ustica in December 1926 and January 1927 were: Marshall's *Principles of Economics* (1890), in the Italian translation by Pasquale Jannaccone,[18] as well as an *Histoire de l'inflation: Le déplacement de la richesse en Europe (1914–1925)*, by Richard Lewinsohn,[19] and the *Corso di scienza della finanza, tenuto nell'Università di Torino e nell'Università Bocconi nel 1925–26* by Einaudi (the text of the lectures given at the Universities of Turin and Milan).[20] Gramsci ordered books from the bookshop, in particular because he wanted to organize a series of multidisciplinary lectures for the political prisoners; he was himself in charge of the literary and historical section.

On 14 January 1927, the military court of Milan issued a warrant for the arrest of Gramsci. On 20 January 1927, the prisoner left the island of Ustica and, on 7 February, he was put in the San Vittore prison in Milan to await trial. Before leaving Ustica, he told his friends there that they could make use of the bookshop account that had been opened in his name, an offer attested to in a letter from Amadeo Bordiga, also a prisoner at Ustica, to Sraffa, dated 27 January 1927.[21] After Gramsci's transfer to Milan, Sraffa went on sending him books; in June, for example, he sent him Antonio Graziadei's recently published *Capitale e colonie*.[22]

During the summer Sraffa asked the examining magistrate's permission to visit Gramsci in prison, claiming that he was a 'school friend' of his. The request was granted, and he was thus able to confirm in person to Gramsci that the unlimited account at the Milan bookshop existed.[23] He immediately informed the Italian Communist Party about the prisoner's situation. He contacted the Italian underground 'Centro Interno' of the party, which was also the occasion of his meeting Camilla Ravera (1889–1988), a member of the political bureau and of the secretariat.[24] But the 'Centro Externo' in exile – first in Switzerland, then in France – was his main contact. At first he was in touch with Angelo Tasca, who had participated in the establishment of *L'Ordine Nuovo*, and who was now in Paris, editing *Lo Stato Operaio*, a new theoretical review which had started up in March 1927. In 1928, Tasca joined the Central Committee of the Italian Communist Party, and became Secretary of the Communist International for Latin countries. Sraffa visited him in Paris at the beginning of September 1927, just before crossing the Channel.[25] As soon as he arrived in London, where he stayed for a few days, he asked Tasca to write a piece for him setting out the condition of the imprisoned philosopher, who was already ill. He intended to translate and possibly revise it, and to have it published in the newspapers, to attract the attention of the English public. He specified that:

> The letter should take the following elements into account: (a) Communism is very unpopular with liberal opinion over here, and consequently the appeal should be purely sentimental, and should not stress the political aspect. English liberals are moved first of all by the life of an animal, then by the life of a man, and finally by that of a Communist; (b) they have already heard a lot about Fascist atrocities, and something special is thus necessary to awaken their consciences; that special thing, in our case, cannot be the personality of our friend, but rather his physical condition and the ill-treatment which is being inflicted upon him.[26]

Tasca accepted, and immediately applied himself to the task.[27] Three days later the text was sent to Sraffa,[28] who had settled in Cambridge and announced on 15 October that he was translating it into English.[29] The text was published only in the *Manchester Guardian* of 24 October 1927, as a letter to the editor, 'The Methods of Fascism: the Case of Antonio Gramsci', signed 'An Italian in England'. It is more than likely that the first sentence of the text was written by Sraffa:

> Sir, – In view of the discussion which has been taking place in your columns on the methods of Fascism, it seems opportune to bring before your readers the facts of a recent case which can hardly be included within Mr Shaw's category of crimes justified by 'necessity'.[30]

The note that followed, written by Angelo Tasca, gave an account of the imprisonment and ill-treatment of Gramsci, emphasizing the steady deterioration of his physical health, not forgetting the threat of a very harsh sentence. The prospects were indeed gloomy, and on 4 June 1928, the Fascist Special Court condemned Gramsci to twenty years, four months and five days in prison. At the time of the trial, Sraffa wrote to newspapers with left-wing sympathies to stir up a 'certain amount of publicity'.[31]

On 19 July 1928, Gramsci was transferred to a prison hospital in Turi, near Bari; he stayed there until December 1933. Gramsci hoped that his sentence would be reviewed, after a petition for a reprieve had been lodged with the Court of Appeal by Umberto Terracini, in the name of the Italian Communist Party. He tried to find out the result of the petition by asking Piero Sraffa to consult his uncle, Senator Mariano D'Amelio, First President of the Court.[32]

Since 1928, the sister-in-law of the prisoner, Tatiana Schucht, had been sending copies or originals of the prisoner's letters to Sraffa, who, in turn, had had them delivered to the General Secretary of the Communist Party, Togliatti.[33] In 1929–30, he was able to meet Camilla Ravera;[34] but she returned to Italy in June 1930 to reconstitute the party's 'Centro Interno', was arrested on 10 July, and sentenced to five years in prison and eight years *confino*. During the same year, Sraffa also lost the contact he had been keeping up since 1927 with Tasca, when the latter was expelled from the party for 'right wing opportunism' in September 1929.[35] Indeed it was at this time that the Italian Communists initiated their famous 'about turn' (*svolta*) by rigidly applying the decisions issuing from the Sixth Congress of the Third International and especially from the Tenth Plenum (July 1929). Political struggle was specially directed against 'Social Fascism' and social democracy. The party declared that a revolutionary situation existed in Italy. Sanctions were enforced against those Communist leaders who disagreed with the new line, in particular against the 'Three': Alfonso Leonetti,[36] Paolo Ravazzoli and Pietro Tresso. Gramsci managed to make his disagreement with the new political orientation known from his prison cell.[37]

Sraffa spent the summer of 1930 in the USSR. He was able to visit Gramsci's wife, Giulia Schucht, who was having a course of treatment in a convalescent home, and her two children. In August he joined Maurice Dobb in Moscow. At the beginning of September, the two friends started on a series of factory visits.[38] On his return from this trip, Sraffa appeared enthusiastic and very confident about the future of the Soviet system.

In 1931, he met Giorgio Amendola (1906–80), who had joined the Communist Party in 1929 and was the son of the celebrated intellectual and liberal politician, Giovanni Amendola. Giorgio Amendola recalls in his memoirs how he was asked by Togliatti, in June 1931, to pick up some of Gramsci's letters from Sraffa's lodgings in Cambridge.[39] It was to be the start of a long friendship. From the summer of 1931 to the summer of 1932, when he passed through Paris, Sraffa gave his new friend (who, as well as holding a PhD in economics was also in charge of the *osservatorio economico* column in the review *Lo Stato Operaio*) a lot of information about the commitment the Banca Commerciale Italiana had made to helping industries that found themselves in difficulties, and about the creation of the Istituto Mobiliare Italiano.[40]

ATTEMPTS AT ORGANIZING DISCUSSIONS WITH THE PRISONER

In August 1931, Gramsci, suffering from Pott's disease, tuberculosis and arteriosclerosis, was going through a difficult time. Sraffa decided to visit him at the prison in Turi. The prison governor, who took his orders from the head of state himself, said that he was willing to authorize the meeting, on condition that Sraffa pressed the prisoner to send a plea for mercy to Mussolini. Sraffa refused, and the visit did not take place.[41]

In February 1929, the prisoner had obtained permission to keep notebooks in his cell, and was allowed to write; at the time he had the idea of working on some specific subjects, including a history of Italian intellectuals, a critique of Croce's philosophy, the principles of 'historical materialism', and an essay on the theme of 'Americanism' and 'Fordism'.[42] None of these projects was in fact to be carried through; the twenty-nine *Prison Notebooks* appear as a series of scattered notes which Gramsci intended to rework and complete. To continue his work, Gramsci ordered some books from the Milan bookshop where he had an account. Sraffa also sent him various periodicals, among which were the annual volumes published by the Banca Commerciale Italiana, *Movimento economico dell'Italia*, as well as the English *Labour Monthly* and *Manchester Guardian Weekly*.[43]

After 1929, Gramsci had also been studying Dante's *Divine Comedy*. He was particularly interested in Canto X of the *Inferno*, about which he wrote several notes. At the beginning of 1931, Sraffa sent Gramsci a biography of Dante by Cosmo,[44] the man who had been responsible for Sraffa's meeting with the founder of *L'Ordine Nuovo* in 1919. In February 1931, Gramsci mentioned to Sraffa, through the agency of Tatiana Schucht, that he would like some news of their former teacher from Turin, who had been forbidden to teach by the Fascists in 1926.[45] Sraffa got in contact with Cosmo, and answered the prisoner's query in a letter dated 10 August 1931.[46] In September, Gramsci contemplated sending his notes on Canto X of the *Inferno* to his old teacher to find out whether or not his interpretation was new.[47] Sraffa sent the notes to Cosmo, who answered on 29 December, confirming, on the whole, the Gramscian interpretation.[48]

On 14 March 1932, Gramsci asked his friend 'if any publications relating to Machiavelli's views on economics and economic policy are in existence', and asked that he try to find for him the essay by Gino Arias, 'Il pensiero economico di Niccolò Machiavelli', published in the *Annali di Economia* of the Bocconi University in 1928. He raised the following problem:

> Can it be said that Machiavelli was a 'mercantilist' – if not in the sense that he consciously thought along mercantilist lines, at any rate in the sense that his political thought corresponded to mercantilism, i. e. that he was saying in political terms what the mercantilists were saying in terms of political economy? Or couldn't it actually be argued that in the political language of Machiavelli (especially in *The Art of War*) we may find the first trace of a Physiocratic conception of the State, and that therefore he might be regarded as a precursor of the French Jacobins...?[49]

Sraffa sent off the article, with his answer, on 21 April.[50] He declared that he knew nothing of Machiavelli's economic thought but that the study by Arias broadly confirmed Gramsci's judgment. He added:

> It seems to me that there is a strong analogy with an English economist of the seventeenth century, William Petty, whom Marx calls 'the founder of classical economy', ... the only reference I have found is in Schmoller, *Lineamenti di economia nazionale*, It. trans., vol. I, p. 239, which mentions a mercantilist Machiavelli.[51]

Gramsci found this answer entirely satisfactory, and never again referred to the theme in his work.[52]

Sraffa tried to persuade Gramsci to review his friend Rodolfo Morandi's book, *Storia della grande industria in Italia*, published in 1931.[53] To encourage him to accept the task, he ventured his own opinion of the work. It seemed to him that:

> the author sees very clearly how one of the bases of the development of industry was the low level of the costs of production, but that he has neglected the links between industry and agriculture, that is to say, the other essential base constituted by the existence of a market outlet con-

> sisting of an economically backward sector exercising a function similar to that of oversea territories as, for example, in the case of England.[54]

The criticism formulated here by Sraffa was slightly 'Luxemburgist', and anticipated, at least in part, numerous analyses of Morandi's book which were to appear in Italy much later, during the sixties.[55] But Gramsci made no comment about the book; in the *Prison Notebooks* he simply transcribed the main passages of a review written by the economist Antonio De Viti de Marco in the *Riforma Sociale*, and rounded them off with a few remarks.[56] Increasingly weakened by illness, he would never be able to return to these questions in his *Notebooks*.

Despite numerous failures, the outlines of a few exchanges of views between the prisoner and Sraffa exist, in the form of dialogues that could not be completed owing to Gramsci's state of health. In Chapter IV we will consider an exchange of views about the philosophical scope of Ricardo's theory, an exchange inaugurated by Gramsci, who was considering the development of 'historical materialism'.[57] In the present chapter we examine two important exchanges which took place despite the bars of the prison, perforce through the mediation of Tatiana Schucht, in 1931 and 1932. The first dealt with the situation of the Jews in Italy, the second with recent developments in the idealist philosophy of Croce.

A DIALOGUE ON THE SITUATION OF THE JEWS IN ITALY

The first of the above-mentioned themes is particularly interesting, both because Sraffa, being Jewish, was personally concerned, and because it took place before the promulgation of Mussolini's racial laws in 1938. The discussion started with a reflection made by Gramsci in a letter to Tatiana Schucht on 28 September 1931:

> there has been no anti-Semitism in Italy for a long while now. Jews can become ministers of the crown (not to mention prime ministers, as in the case of Luzzatti); they can also reach the rank of general in the army. Marriages of Jews with Christians are very numerous, particularly in the large cities; and this is not only a working-class phenomenon, for a number of girls of the aristocracy have married Jewish intellectuals.[58]

Some time later, Sraffa offered his point of view:

> what he says about the Jews in Italy is not entirely true nowadays. On the one hand, since the Concordat, they have been granted certain privileges as religious communities, in the form of a certain degree of legal recognition of Jewish universities, which have been authorized to receive contributions from members, etc. ; all the old rabbis and the young

> Zionists are very pleased by this. On the other hand, they are barred, *de facto* if not *de jure*, from certain posts; it is well known, for example, that Jews cannot enter the Italian Academy (certain Fascists of world-wide fame have also been excluded); they are barred from Parliament, where the only Jew is Olivetti, Secretary to the Confederation of Industry; and I believe that for quite a few years none of them has been appointed to the position of senator: it is said, however, that an exception will soon be made in favour of Morpurgo, of Assicurazioni Generali, for special reasons. Both tendencies, although they may appear opposed, evidently aim at forcing the Jews back into a segregated community.[59]

The prisoner replied to this analysis on 8 February 1932:

> I don't think the inference is justified that there is an 'evident' tendency to 'force the Jews back into an isolated community'; this tendency seems to me to be rather the 'subjective' one of the old rabbis and of the young Zionists. The objective truth seems to be that, as a result of the Concordat, the Jews are in the same position as Protestants. On the other hand there does exist – or will exist – a social category whose condition is very sad in comparison with that of Jews and Protestants: and that will be (or rather is already) the category of unfrocked priests and monks. These latter will be excluded from employment by the State; that is, they will be degraded as citizens. The fact that it has been possible to give the sanction of law to the institution of such a category of civil pariahs seems to me much more important than the status in law of Jews and Protestants – to whom legal prerogatives have been granted that are the very reverse of degrading, in the spirit of the law.
>
> I do not rule out the possibility that an anti-Semitic tendency may yet develop here; I do not see that it exists today... .
>
> And so the line drawn by the Academy and Parliament proves nothing: scientists of world fame who are not Jews have found and will find themselves on the wrong side of it.[60]

Sraffa expressed his disagreement with this line of argument in a letter forwarded by Tatiana Schucht on 18 March 1932;[61] Gramsci in turn reasserted his position one last time on 21 March, declaring:

> What I wished to establish is this: that for some time now no popular anti-Semitism ... has existed in Italy.[62]

THE EXCHANGE OF VIEWS ABOUT BENEDETTO CROCE'S IDEALIST PHILOSOPHY

In August 1931, Sraffa advised his friend to finish his work on the history of

Italian intellectuals as quickly as possible. While announcing that he was sending him a copy of the Soviet contributions to the second International Congress of the History of Science and Technology, which had taken place in London in June and July, under the title of Science at the Crossroads,[63] he attempted to begin a discussion on Italian intellectuals' lack of interest in scientific questions:

> It is a curious fact that all educated Italians suffer from a cultural blind spot: ignorance of the natural sciences. Croce is an extreme but typical case. The philosophers believe that, when they have finally proved that scientists are incapable of doing philosophy, their mission will have been accomplished. And thus the natural sciences have been left in the care of the Positivists, with the results that we all know. Lately, a few scientists, at least in England, seem to have abandoned Positivism in order to give themselves over to some kind of vulgar mysticism.[64]

This reflection is important. The Italian 'neo-idealism' of the early twentieth century was part of an international movement of 'idealist reaction against science', and related to various anti-rationalist currents. According to Croce, science belonged to the domain of 'pseudo-concepts'. Given these attitudes, Italy did not join in the important debates about epistemology and the history of the sciences in the first third of the twentieth century. The cultural background was not to change until after the Second World War and the collapse of the Fascist regime.

Gramsci was very ill during the summer of 1931, and during that period was unable to work at imposing some order on the numerous fragments of his *Notebooks*. In the spring of 1932 Sraffa – in an attempt to encourage him to continue his work – decided to ask him to write reviews of some books. His first choice was Croce's *Storia d'Europa nel secolo XIX*, which had just been published,[65] and which had been preceded in 1928 by the *Storia d'Italia dal 1871 al 1915*. Gramsci accepted and, on 18 April 1932, sent his first review. In it he examined Croce's role among Italian intellectuals, and posed the problem of 'intellectual and moral struggle'. Concerning Croce's international standing, he remarked that:

> Before the war Croce already held a very high place in the estimation of intellectual circles in all countries. The interesting thing is that – notwithstanding the general opinion – his fame was greater in the English-speaking countries than in Germany or Austria; the editions of his books translated into English are most numerous – larger than the figure for Germany, and indeed for Italy itself. Croce, as is clear from his writings, has a high conception of this position of his as a leader of world culture, and of the responsibilities and duties it carries with it. It's evident

> that his writings presuppose a world public, an élite. It should be remembered that in the final years of the last century Croce's writings on the theory of history provided the two greatest 'revisionist' movements of the time with their intellectual weapons: Eduard Bernstein's in Germany and Sorel's in France. Bernstein has himself admitted that he was compelled to re-elaborate the whole of his philosophic and economic thought after reading Croce's essays. Sorel's close link with Croce was known, but it was not properly appreciated how constant and intimate it was until after the publication of Sorel's letters: in these Sorel reveals throughout his intellectual subordination to Croce in a most surprising manner.
>
> But Croce has carried his revisionist activity still further, during the course of the war, and especially after 1917. The new series of essays on the theory of history begins after 1910 with the essay *Cronache, storie e false storie* and continues right up to the last chapters of the *Storia della storiografia italiana nel secolo XIX*, to the essays on political science and on to the very last literary works – including the *History of Europe* (or so it seems from those chapters which I've read). I think that Croce regards this position of his – as a leader of revisionism – as the most important thing of all, and that he intends the best of his present output to be seen against this background.[66]

Sraffa found this extremely interesting, and decided to ask Gramsci further questions about Croce's work. He asked him to indicate:

> the precise development of Croce's position in relation to the materialist conception of history, and to explain the reasons for the most recent phase of complete and absolute opposition, which appears between his *Storia d'Italia* and his *Storia d'Europa*. How is this latest development linked to Croce's complete change after his break with Gentile? Would it be correct to say that he has been forced to take refuge in the 'religion of liberty' and such-like fantasies to hide the fact that, for him and his friends, the ground has been cut from under their feet, without any hope of ever retrieving it?[67]

However, he preferred to wait for the end of the review to begin a real dialogue with Gramsci. The latter continued this work in his letters of 25 April, 2 and 9 May. On 2 May 1932, he commented:

> I have already alluded to the great importance which Croce attaches to his theoretical revisionist activity, and mentioned how, on his own explicit admission, the whole purport of his thought in the last twenty years has been directed towards the end of completing the revision and turning it

> into a liquidation... . Today he has given literary form to what he calls ethico-political history: the *History of Europe* is intended to be exemplary. In what does Croce's innovation consist? Has it the significance which he attributes to it, and above all has it this 'liquidating' quality which he asserts that it possesses ?
>
> One definite observation that we may make is that Croce, in his historico-political activity, lays stress exclusively on that moment which in politics is called 'hegemony' by consent, i.e. by virtue of cultural direction, as distinct from the moment of force, of restraint, of State intervention through the law and the police. It's honestly hard to understand how Croce can believe in the capacity of this conception of historical theory to achieve a definition liquidating of any and every philosophy of praxis. In the very same period in which Croce was shaping this so-called 'club'[68] of his, the greatest modern theorists of the philosophy of praxis were doing the job of shaping a much more efficient instrument; they were engaged in a systematic revaluation of the concept of the moment of 'hegemony' or cultural direction in opposition to the mechanistic and fatalistic conceptions of 'economism'.[69]

On 9 May 1932, he added:

> As I haven't yet read the *History of Europe*, I obviously can't comment on its actual content. What I can do, though, is to jot down a few observations which might seem to lie outside the subject under discussion, but in fact do not, as you shall see ... It seems to me that Croce's history can only be called 'speculative' or 'philosophic' history, not ethico-political history: it is for this reason, and not because it is ethico-political, that it is in opposition to historical materialism... .
>
> But his philosophy is a 'speculative' philosophy, and because this is its nature it is bound to perpetuate the theological and the transcendental, though clothing these in the language of historicism... .
>
> In connection with this point there is another observation I have to make; it more closely concerns the *History of Europe*, as regards both conception and composition.
>
> Can you envisage a unitary history of Europe starting in 1815, i.e. with the Restoration? If a history of Europe is to be written so as to describe the formation of an historic bloc, it cannot exclude the French Revolution and the Napoleonic Wars, which are the 'economic-juridical' premise of the historic European bloc, the moment of force and struggle. Croce takes as his subject the subsequent moment, that in which the forces previously let loose have reached a state of equilibrium – or, – to put it differently, have undergone a catharsis; he makes this moment a fact existing in and

for itself, and so constructs his paradigm of history. He did the same thing with the *History of Italy* ... .
Croce, contradicting himself, confuses 'liberty' *qua* philosophical principle or speculative concept with liberty *qua* ideology – that is, an instrument of practical government, an element of moral unity sustaining a hegemony. If the whole of history is the history of liberty, or in other words of the spirit which creates itself (and in this jargon liberty equals spirit, spirit equals history and history equals liberty), why should the history of nineteenth century Europe alone be singled out as the history of liberty?[70]

He replied to Sraffa's questions on 6 June 1932. He began by pointing out that certain elements of an answer were contained in the letter of 18 April, where he had been dealing with Croce's position during the war. However, he added the following:

The break with Gentile took place in 1912, and it was Gentile who broke away from Croce and tried to achieve his philosophical independence. I don't think that Croce has changed his position from that time onwards, although he has since defined his doctrines with greater precision. A more notable change is the one which took place between 1900 and 1910. The so-called 'religion of liberty' is not a discovery of recent years, it is the recapitulation, in a single drastic formula, of the entire sweep of his thought right from the moment he abandoned Catholicism. He himself admits this in his intellectual biography (*Contributo alla critica di me stesso*).
Nor does Gentile seem to me in disagreement with him over this point either. I think that your interpretation of the formula 'religion of liberty' is inaccurate, as you give it a mystical content (or so one might think, seeing that you talk about 'taking refuge' in this religion as if it were a question of a 'flight' from the world, etc.). It's got nothing to do with that at all. Religion of liberty simply means faith in modern civilization, which has no need of the transcendental or of revelations, and contains in itself its own rationality and its own origin. Therefore it's an anti-mystical formula or, if you like, an anti-religious one. In Croce's eyes every conception of the world and every philosophy *is* a 'religion', in so far as it becomes a norm of living, a moral code. Religions in the confessional sense are of course 'religions' as well, but 'mythological' ones and therefore in a certain sense inferior – it's as if they corresponded to the historical childhood of the human race. The origins of this doctrine are already to be found in Hegel and in Vico, and are a common patrimony of the whole of Italian idealist philosophy, Gentile's as well as Croce's. Gentile's scholastic reform is based on this doctrine, so far as religious

> instruction in schools is concerned. Gentile himself wanted to allow religious teaching only in the elementary schools (to restrict it, that is, to the years of actual childhood), and even the government did not want it to be included in the curriculum of the senior classes.
>
> And so I am inclined to believe that you are exaggerating the extent of Croce's isolation at the present time. He is not as isolated as you think. Don't allow yourself to be taken in by the polemical effervescence of writers who are all to a greater or lesser extent irresponsible dilettanti.[71]

Gramsci was thus able to give his friend some parts of an answer to the question concerning Croce's links with Marxism, and to the question of 'religion of liberty'. He still had not read the *Storia d'Europa*, which he was to review, but he knew the contents of the first three chapters, which had been published separately the previous year. So he did not give any verdict on the 'complete and absolute opposition' between the *Storia d'Italia* and the *Storia d'Europa*. Sraffa, for his part, sent a letter to Tatiana Schucht on 21 June 1932 in which he expressed his thoughts about the reviews as a whole.[72] He claimed to have understood perfectly the developments bearing on, for example, cultural hegemony, in the letters of April and May. In Gramsci's reflections on Croce's role among Italian intellectuals contained in his letter of 18 April Sraffa seems to have recognized a concept that already existed, though in an embryonic state, in one of the prisoner's previous works, which he did not name for reasons of prudence. He did, though, refer implicitly to *Alcuni temi della questione meridionale* (October 1926), which had never been finished because of Gramsci's arrest, but had been published by the Italian Communist Party in 1930, and in which the author mentioned, among other things, that:

> Giustino Fortunato and Benedetto Croce represent the keystones of the meridionalist system and, in a certain sense, are the two main figures of Italian reactionism.

Gramsci explained at the time that these two thinkers were the representatives of an 'intellectual bloc' which operated in the Mezzogiorno as a stratum 'above the agrarian bloc'.[73] Sraffa went on to ask his friend further questions. Why did Croce have such success in English-speaking countries, compared with Germany? What was the source of Gramsci's information concerning the remark made by Eduard Bernstein, the author of the *Die Voraussetzungen des Sozialismus und die Aufgaben der Sozialdemokratie*,[74] about Croce? Sraffa did not in fact know that Gramsci was referring implicitly to a declaration made by Bernstein to Sorel, which was mentioned in a letter Sorel wrote to Croce on 9 September 1899, and published in *La Critica* in 1927.[75] Finally, he said he was surprised by the comment that Croce had had a strong influence on Sorel: 'if one considers that, intellectually, Sorel was a disciple of Renan and had an extreme antipathy for Hegel', it might be thought that Sorel's influence on Croce was much stronger than the contrary, and thus he asked for clarification on this point.[76]

Sorel did indeed owe much to Ernest Renan's philosophy of history, and, in 1906, devoted to it *Le Système historique de Renan*,[77] in which he indicated that the method best adapted to the study of historical phenomena originated from psychology. When discussing the problem of the relationship between Croce and Sorel, which had been posed by Gramsci and Sraffa, it must be mentioned that this relationship continued from 1896 until 1921, that was infinitely more complex than the straightforward dependence of the one upon the other, and that it should be divided into different periods.

This discussion between the imprisoned philosopher and the intellectual living in Cambridge might seem to have been promising, but unfortunately it was interrupted as early as June 1932, owing to a further deterioration in the state of Gramsci's health in August and September.

THE CAMPAIGN FOR GRAMSCI'S RELEASE; LAST MEETINGS WITH THE PRISONER

In September 1932 Gramsci's sister-in-law petitioned the prison authorities to allow a doctor to visit the prisoner. The request was granted in February 1933. Professor Umberto Arcangeli's diagnosis was very pessimistic, and he recommended that the Communist leader be transferred urgently 'to a civil hospital or to a private clinic, if he cannot be granted a conditional release'.[78] Shortly afterwards, an international campaign was mounted to try to obtain Gramsci's release. In June 1933, an 'international committee' was set up in Paris around such figures as Romain Rolland, Henri Barbusse and Paul Langevin. Sraffa gave the Italian Communist Party the certificate drawn up by Professor Arcangeli; this document was mysteriously published on 8 May in *L'Humanité*. Sraffa was entirely against such a move, which was likely to jeopardize the prisoner's situation,[79] since steps had already been taken to try to obtain his release.

Gramsci refused to ask Mussolini for a pardon, believing that such a demand would be tantamount to moral suicide. Paolo Spriano mentions that Gramsci had two strategies in mind at the beginning of 1933: the first was to obtain a 'conditional release' from the Fascist authorities; the second to encourage a Soviet initiative aimed at an exchange of prisoners between the USSR and Italy.[80] Sraffa played an important role in both approaches. Concerning the first, it must be mentioned that, on the occasion of the tenth anniversary of the 'March on Rome', in October 1932, the Fascists had decided to reduce the prisoner's sentence to twelve years and four months in prison. Gramsci felt that under these circumstances a request for conditional release might be successful, and suggested that advice on this score might be obtained through Sraffa's uncle, Mariano D'Amelio, First President of the Court of Appeal. Sraffa had been working in this direction since the beginning of 1933, with the consent of Gramsci's family (notably Tatiana Schucht and Carlo Gramsci, Antonio's brother) and of the Italian Communist Party. His father Angelo also played a part: one of his colleagues, the lawyer Saverio Castellet, prepared the prisoner's requests to the Special Court. Nothing, however, was to come of this. The second approach also came to nothing, as no agreement was ever reached between Italy and the USSR for an exchange of prisoners.[81]

Yet Gramsci managed, in the autumn, to get himself transferred to the clinic of Dr C. Cusumano in Formia and thus left the prison of Turi, near Bari, in December. Sraffa took care of the cost of the prison hospital where Gramsci was held from December 1933 to July 1935. He was given permission to stay one week with the prisoner four or five times a year.[82] Very little is in fact known about the conversations which took place between the two friends and which were free from police surveillance: economic questions, world political events, news ... but most probably there were none of the detailed in-depth discussions such as were found in their correspondence.[83] In September 1934, the request for conditional release, again presented by the prisoner, was finally granted, partly because of the international campaign on his behalf. Nevertheless he kept his status as political prisoner. In August 1935 he was transferred to the Quisisana clinic in Rome where Sraffa visited him under the same conditions as at Formia. Again we know very little about the subjects of the conversations they had when they were alone, although political activity in Italy and elsewhere was particularly intense at that time. In October 1935 Italy invaded Abyssinia; in 1936 the Popular Front won the elections in France, and civil war broke out in Spain. Not long afterwards, disquieting trials were begun in Moscow, involving the Bolshevik leaders. Sraffa discussed these conversations with Paolo Spriano in 1967 and on various occasions afterwards. He mentioned that:

> Gramsci avoided taking an open stand about a whole series of burning questions, in particular those which concerned the political struggle that was taking place in the USSR; he preferred listening rather than expressing his own opinions.[84]

However, he revealed to Alfonso Leonetti and his companion Pia Carena that Gramsci had one day talked to him about the Moscow trials and had said that 'confessions do not constitute proof'.[85]

Sraffa met Gramsci for the last time in the Quisisana clinic in Rome, on 25 March 1937. The prisoner now knew that he would officially be free on

20 April, and he was considering where he would live in the future. He had at first thought of returning to his native village in Sardinia, but later considered emigrating to the USSR, to rejoin his wife, of whose health he knew nothing. He discussed this latter option with Sraffa, who wrote the emigration request for him, sending him the document on 18 April.[86] During their last meeting, Gramsci gave his friend an important piece of political advice to be forwarded to the leadership of the Communist Party. Since 1930–32, he had been thinking about the strategy that should be adopted after the fall of Fascism; his position had evolved considerably since the debate he had had with Sraffa in 1924. The most likely hypothesis, according to him, was that it would not be possible to pass directly from Fascism to Socialism; a transition period would be necessary. Therefore, the only realistic rallying point was to be a 'Constituent Assembly'; the Italian Communist Party would have to join forces on this basis with the other anti-fascist parties.[87]

And so, on 25 March, Gramsci passed on the following message: 'The Popular Front in Italy is the Constituent Assembly'; Sraffa immediately communicated it to Togliatti through the agency of the latter's brother-in-law, Mario Montagnana, member of the leadership of the Italian Communist party in Paris.[88]

PRESERVING THE *PRISON NOTEBOOKS*

After Gramsci's death (27 April 1937), Tatiana Schucht managed to recover the *Prison Notebooks* and, on 12 May, she gave an exact account of the prisoner's last moments in a letter to Sraffa:

> First of all, I want you to write to me whether you think it is useful, or, rather, absolutely necessary, that you put Nino's manuscripts in order. Clearly, only someone competent should undertake this work.[89]

Sraffa passed this document on to the 'Centro Externo' of the Communist Party, suggesting that the *Notebooks* be handed over to the prisoner's wife, Giulia, in the USSR. The party leadership gave its assent.[90] Sraffa wrote to Tatiana Schucht on 25 May:

> I have been thinking about what you said of the M[anuscript]s, and have come to the conclusion that the best solution would be to send them all to Giulia, who will take proper care of them. You will naturally wait until you have an absolutely safe means of transmission; and if this is at the moment impossible, you will wait for a favourable occasion.[91]

It was therefore advisable to transfer the *Prison Notebooks* to a safe place as soon as possible. Sraffa immediately contacted his anti-fascist friend Mattioli, managing director of the Banca Commerciale Italiana since 1933, to find a suitable place. The manuscripts were deposited, probably in a safe deposit box at the head office of the bank in Rome, on 6 July.[92] Beforehand, on 20 May, Palmiro Togliatti had asked Sraffa to inform him of the directions he had been given by Gramsci about the *Notebooks*, and especially concerning their publication. His letter contains a telling remark:

> The task of protecting Antonio's political and literary legacy is too important to be left to our occasional meetings.[93]

He also asked Sraffa's advice about possible publication of extracts from the *Prison Letters*. Sraffa answered him, in a letter which was subsequently lost, with a brief description of the various manuscripts, but declared that he had not been given any precise instructions about them. Tatiana Schucht, external assistant to the Soviet embassy in Rome, managed to have the *Prison Notebooks* sent to the USSR, and they arrived in Moscow in July 1938.

After the Second World War and the fall of Fascism, Gramsci's work was finally published. Giulio Einaudi – the son of Luigi Einaudi – published the *Prison Letters* in Turin in 1947 and, between 1948 and 1951, the *Prison Notebooks*, in six volumes, arranged according to themes chosen by the General Secretary of the Italian Communist Party, Palmiro Togliatti. The definitive and complete edition of the *Notebooks*, without any *a priori* grouping, only came out in 1975, edited by Valentino Gerratana.

Sraffa had no ongoing contact with revolutionary militants after the war. His trips to Italy were less and less frequent. During these trips, he managed to meet the same major party activists whom he had met in the twenties and thirties. In Rome, he once more met the General Secretary, Togliatti, but also Giorgio Amendola and Alfonso Leonetti. During the sixties he was consulted by Italian researchers who wanted to find out more about his friendship with Gramsci. The historian Paolo Spriano, author of the seminal *Storia del Partito Comunista Italiano*,[94] saw him at length in Rome, in 1967. He was later to say:

> About the most delicate issues concerning Gramsci's political differences of opinions with the ruling group of the Party between 1930 and 1934 Sraffa said nothing. He listened to the questions, and showed interest in evidence from other sources, but added nothing new to what had already been proven by the test of time.[95]

In 1974, Sraffa decided to hand over to the Gramsci Foundation many letters from Tatiana Schucht and various documents that he had carefully kept in Cambridge.

The Italian Communist Party, during the sixties, offered to facilitate his return to Italy and to appoint him Honorary President of the Gramsci Institute in Rome. Sraffa declined the offer. Later, in 1975, through Giorgio Napolitano, the Communist Party again offered to pay the costs of moving to Italy, and to ensure that his life would be as quiet as in Trinity College. In a letter of 22 April 1975, he declared himself to be very touched by the offer, but refused it, pleading that his state of health did not permit him to consider such a move.[96]

Piero Sraffa and Antonio Gramsci were at their closest in the thirties. It will now be necessary to examine Sraffa's first ten years in Cambridge and the new contacts he made there.

3 First years in Cambridge

THE CAMBRIDGE LECTURES: BRIEF BUT FRUITFUL

As the Fascist regime was steadily increasing the level of political repression, Sraffa decided not to pursue an academic career in Italy – although he had recently been awarded a professorship at Cagliari – and instead accepted Keynes's offer to teach in Britain. When he arrived in Cambridge at the end of September 1927, Keynes personally helped him to settle in, finding him accommodation in the college building (17b St Edward's Passage) in which he himself had a flat and where he stayed with his wife Lydia for weekends in Cambridge. Even though Sraffa was not (nor would he ever be made) a Fellow of King's College, Keynes arranged high-table dining rights for him.

Keynes had suggested to his friend that, starting in 1927–28, he might take charge of three courses of lectures: an advanced course on the theory of value, a course on the theory of distribution, and a course in applied economics dealing with the 'Problems of Public Finance as handled by Continental Economists and with special reference to continental practice'.[1]

Sraffa immediately accepted the first and third of these propositions, but said that he had nothing original to contribute on the subject of distribution. When he arrived in Cambridge, he asked Keynes whether his teaching could not be postponed for a few months, to give him time to improve his command of English. Keynes accepted and, in the autumn of 1928, Sraffa started a course on the history of theories of value called 'Advanced Theory of Value', and a course on the banking systems of Italy and Germany.[2] He felt ill at ease when he had to speak in public – especially to give lectures – and spent a very long time preparing his lectures.

In his course on theories of value, Sraffa developed a critique of Marshall's *Principles of Economics*, and developed the ideas he had introduced in the 1926 *Economic Journal* article. His attacks on Marshallian orthodoxy often shocked the majority of his students, and very few of them derived much benefit from the lectures; those who did included Richard Ferdinand

Kahn (born 1903) and Joan Robinson (1903–83). In her 'Reminiscences' (1977),[3] she noted:

> He was calmly committing the sacrilege of pointing out inconsistencies in Marshall, and, moreover, introducing us to rather contemporary schools of thought (but they were no better).

Kahn became a close friend of Sraffa's in 1929.[4] The same year, Kahn wrote his doctoral thesis. Influenced by Marshall's *Principles*, he had chosen to study 'the economics of the short period'; and his choice had been approved by Keynes. He was also encouraged by Gerald F. Shove and Sraffa. Kahn had numerous 'long conversations' with Sraffa, and was able to use a certain amount of material from these in his thesis, which was defended at the University of Cambridge in December 1929; he also used Sraffa's 1926 article in his seventh chapter, on 'market imperfection', and was given direct help with the section on duopoly.[5]

Joan Robinson, who began teaching at the University of Cambridge in 1931, owed much to the innovative elements of Sraffa's lectures. Her first book, *The Economics of Imperfect Competition* (1933), although strongly influenced by Pigou's work, was 'inspired by a hint from Sraffa'. In the foreword she went as far as to say:

> Of more recent work, my chief debt is to Mr Piero Sraffa's article in the *Economic Journal* of December 1926 .... Mr Sraffa's article must be regarded as the fount from which my work flows, for the chief aim of this book is to attempt to carry out his pregnant suggestion that the whole theory of value should be treated in terms of monopoly analysis.[6]

Sraffa had many discussions with Joan Robinson, but most of the criticisms he made were negative.

At the beginning of 1930, Keynes had decided to bring together Dennis H. Robertson, Gerald F. Shove and Sraffa for a symposium on the 1926 theses; the material was published in March in the *Economic Journal*, under the title 'Increasing Returns and the Representative Firm'.[7] In his paper, 'The Trees of the Forest', Robertson tried to defend Marshall. During the discussion, Sraffa noted that:

> [this] theory cannot be interpreted in a way which makes it logically self-consistent and, at the same time, reconciles it with the facts it sets out to explain. Mr. Robertson's remedy is to discard mathematics, and he suggests that my remedy is to discard the facts; perhaps I ought to have explained that, in the circumstances, I think it is Marshall's theory that should be discarded.[8]

Joseph Schumpeter tried to contribute to the debate in a letter to Sraffa dated

3 May 1930, which, to Sraffa's regret, had not been sent to the *Economic Journal* as a 'letter to the editor'.[9]

In the autumn of 1930, Sraffa decided to resign from his lectureship. For months he had been in constant anguish about having to deliver his ideas in public, and about the rather 'unorthodox' nature of these ideas, especially those in the course on the history of the theories of values. When reminiscing about that period, Austin Robinson, Joan Robinson's husband, said that:

> He found the strain of lecturing almost intolerable (he would sit up all night before a lecture worrying about what he was going to say).[10]

Sraffa told Keynes, as well as Austin Robinson, who was in charge of the organization of the economics courses at Cambridge, that he wanted to stop lecturing and return to Italy.[11] Keynes, who did not want to see his friend leave King's College, took it upon himself to find a solution to this delicate problem. In 1931 he obtained for Sraffa the recently created post of Librarian at the Marshall Library of Economics,[12] a post Sraffa held until 1973. Keynes also had created, especially for Sraffa, a Directorship of Research at King's College: Sraffa was to be in general charge of research students in economics, to find supervisors for their theses, and so on. Towards the end of the thirties, Sraffa asked to be demoted to Assistant Director of Research, in order to have more time for his own research, and held this post until 1963.

As Director of Research, Sraffa organized a seminar during which papers were read by research students. Around 1936 he gave much advice to the young Canadian Lorie Tarshis in the preparation of his doctoral thesis, 'The Determinants of Labour Income', dealing with the share of wages in national income, and with the determinants of the real wage.[13] Sraffa was at the time very interested in the neo-classical theory of wages, about which two important books had recently been published in Britain: John R. Hicks's *The Theory of Wages*[14] and Pigou's *The Theory of Unemployment*.[15] In 1938 he gave advice to one of Keynes's students, John Thomas Dunlop (born 1914), who showed him the draft of an article which was to be published in the *Economic Journal*: 'The Movement of Real and Money Wage Rates'.[16]

In 1939, Robertson resigned from his post at Trinity College to teach at the London School of Economics, where he occupied the chair vacated by T. E. Gregory, who had been appointed consultant of the Indian Reserve Bank. Sraffa succeeded Robertson at the end of the year, thus becoming a Fellow of Trinity College.

HIS FRIENDS IN CAMBRIDGE: DOBB, RAMSEY, WITTGENSTEIN, KEYNES

Sraffa was initiated into the peculiarities of academic life in Cambridge as early as 1927, when he was received into the Political Economy Club, a group which had been reconstituted by Keynes and given new rules.[17] Seminars of the 'Keynes Club', as it came to be known, were held every Monday evening at King's College, in Keynes's rooms and were attended by teachers and a few students. There Sraffa met some fascinating people, several of whom became close friends of his.

First, he renewed his acquaintance with Maurice Dobb (1900–76), who had been a lecturer at the Cambridge Faculty of Economics since 1924. It is difficult to ascertain the date of their first meeting, although it is known that Dobb had been invited to stay in the Sraffa household at Rapallo in the spring of 1925, and had been able to read the manuscript of the essay *Sulle relazioni fra costo e quantità prodotta*, before it was published in November of the same year.[18] Dobb had been a student in Cambridge from 1919 to 1922, and at the London School of Economics from 1923 to 1924. His doctoral thesis, under the supervision of Edwin Cannan, dealt with the theory of capitalist enterprise,[19] and was later published as a book, *Capitalist Enterprise and Social Progress*,[20] in which he tried to reconcile the Marxist theory of surplus value with Marshall's. Dobb had studied the Italian debates on Marxism (Loria, Labriola, Croce, Sorel, etc.) in detail and had been active in the British Communist Party since 1922. It was most probably through him that Sraffa, for reasons unknown, contacted Harry Pollitt, General Secretary of the party from 1929 to 1956.[21]

Sraffa also became a friend of the brilliant young philosopher, logician and mathematician Frank Ramsey (1903–30), who was a friend of Keynes, and had criticized the latter's *A Treatise on Probability*, written in 1914–20 but published only in 1921. In 1923, Ramsey published a lengthy review of Wittgenstein's *Tractatus Logico-philosophicus* in *Mind*; in his 1925 essay, *The Foundations of Mathematics*, published posthumously, he attempted to reconcile the propositions of the *Tractatus* with those developed by Bertrand Russell and Alfred North Whitehead in the *Principia Mathematica* (1910 and 1913). Through Keynes he was accepted into the secret society called the 'Apostles', which had a maximum membership of twelve. He was a Fellow in mathematics of King's College, but was encouraged by Keynes to take an interest also in economics. He wrote two studies, both published in the *Economic Journal*: 'A Contribution to the Theory of Taxation' (March 1927) and 'A Mathematical Theory of Saving' (December 1928). The latter, as Henri Bartoli notes, is particularly important:

> Fifty years ago, F. P. Ramsey showed himself to be a pioneer when he formulated for the first time the problem of optimum growth in intertemporal terms, i. e. the search for the optimum trajectories of the rate of capital accumulation for a given interval of time and for a given economic

system. His work remained almost unknown until the fifties, when Solow, Samuelson and Tinbergen resumed work on the same problems, while adopting Ramsey's methodology, thus generating a great deal of debate.[22]

In 1929, Sraffa met a friend of Ramsey and Keynes, the Austrian-born philosopher Ludwig Wittgenstein (1889–1951), then living in Cambridge. Wittgenstein was a Fellow of Trinity College from 1930 to 1935; like Ramsey, he was a member of the 'Apostles'. Wittgenstein enjoyed the endless philosophical discussions he had with Sraffa, and the latter's criticism led Wittgenstein to abandon the theses of the *Tractatus Logico-philosophicus* and look for new paths, which he developed in *The Blue Book* (1933–34) and, especially, in the first part of *Philosophical Investigations* (1936–45). About Sraffa's influence on Wittgenstein, Georg Henrik von Wright remarked:

> He said that his discussions with Sraffa made him feel like a tree from which all branches had been cut.[23]

In the introduction to *Philosophical Investigations*, Wittgenstein stated:

> I was helped to realize these mistakes – to a degree which I myself am hardly able to estimate – by the criticism which my ideas encountered from Frank Ramsey, with whom I discussed them in the last years of his life. Even more than to this – always certain and forcible – criticism I am indebted to that which a teacher of this university, Mr. P. Sraffa, for many years unceasingly practised on my thoughts. I am indebted to *this* stimulus for the most consequential ideas of this book.[24]

Later, during some conversations which took place in the sixties, Sraffa considerably played down his influence on Wittgenstein's later intellectual development.

In the early thirties, Keynes and Sraffa became close friends. They were both very fond of rare books, with a special predilection for eighteenth century works of philosophy and political economy, and they often spent their Saturdays doing the rounds of the Cambridge antiquarian bookshops, especially the shop of the elderly and celebrated dealer Gustave David (who died in 1936).[25] Schumpeter, who had started teaching at Harvard in 1939, but came back to Cambridge every year, recalled Keynes saying that Sraffa 'became to him [i. e. to Keynes] a much appreciated ally'.[26] One particular event illustrates their common passion: around 1937, Geoffrey Keynes, also a bibliophile, gave his brother John Maynard an extremely rare edition of the *Abstract of Hume's Treatise of Human Nature*, published in 1740 and attributed to the young Adam Smith. Keynes and Sraffa managed to establish not long afterwards that this work had in fact been written by David Hume himself; together they wrote an introduction for the publication of the work in 1938.[27]

PIERO SRAFFA, CRITIC OF KEYNES: FROM THE *TREATISE ON MONEY* TO THE *GENERAL THEORY*

Between 1924 and 1928, Keynes was working on a book whose title changed incessantly in the course of his research: *The Standard of Value* became *The Monetary Standard*, and finally *A Treatise on Money*. Not long after Sraffa had arrived in Britain, Keynes asked him to read some of the drafts, and Sraffa made some critical comments. The correspondence between Keynes and his wife shows, for example, that an important discussion about the book took place on 2 March 1928.[28] Some of these comments were taken into consideration, but it is difficult to determine exactly what Sraffa really thought about the book. According to Joan Robinson, he was 'secretly sceptical' about the originality of the *Treatise on Money*, but her judgment is very different from those expressed by other witnesses. In September 1931, Sraffa confided indirectly in his friend Gramsci, when he sent him the report of the Macmillan Committee, the Committee of Inquiry on Finance and Industry, which had been created by the Labour government in 1929, and sat until 1931; its main members were Keynes, Reginald McKenna, Theodore E. Gregory, R. H. Brand and Ernest Bevin. Sraffa said of the Macmillan Report that:

> Most of it was written by Keynes, and entirely inspired by him. It contains an analysis which throws much light on the causes of the present financial crisis in Great Britain; moreover, it contains a partial exposition of the theory of money and crises that Keynes has put forward, in very tangled and confused language, in his recent *Treatise on Money* (1930). This theory ascribes such crises to an excess of 'saving', in the form of money 'put aside' by savers, over 'investments' in the sense of new constructions, etc., with the result that the money available to acquire everyday commodities is insufficient to cover their production costs. Obviously, much of this is old stuff, though a little of it is new. But Keynes, who strictly speaking was criticizing the liberal capitalist economy, concludes with a defence of the capitalist entrepreneur and a search for 'remedies'.[29]

The 'credit cycle' theory put forward in the *Treatise on Money*[30] was very much in evidence in the report, and also in the views that Keynes expressed during the various sittings of the committee.[31] Sraffa found out, while reading the proofs of the preface of the *Treatise*, dated August 1929, that the author was going to express his thanks to him as well as to Ramsey and Kahn for their stimulating criticisms. Being modest, he told Keynes he did not want to be mentioned; so the preface, which was published in October 1930, does not include his name.[32]

According to Joan Robinson,[33] Sraffa was the first to suggest to his economist friends that they form a working group to study and criticize the *Treatise on Money*. The famous 'Cambridge Circus' was set up at the end of 1930, and lasted until May 1931. The main speakers at this discussion group of young researchers were Kahn, who had been elected to a fellowship at King's in March 1930, James E. Meade, Fellow of Hertford College, Oxford, who was on a year's leave at Trinity, as well as Joan Robinson and her husband Austin, and Sraffa himself. Among the less prominent members were Charles H. P. Gifford, Wynne Plumptre and Lorie Tarshis. Some students doing their third and last year also took part in a few of the meetings. The results of each meeting's debates were given to Keynes during the following weekend[34] by the secretary, R. F. Kahn, who relayed Keynes's comments to the group at the next meeting.[35] A letter of 9 May 1931 from Sraffa to Keynes made reference to the 'Circus'.[36] These stimulating discussions contributed actively to the preparation and maturing of the *General Theory* (1936). Few accounts exist of the impression that Sraffa made during these discussions between economists. In Austin Robinson's words:

> in all our discussions I remember him as much more like a kettle on a slow gas-ring. One waited hopefully for it to boil. When one had almost forgotten, it suddenly came to the boil. Piero Sraffa at full pressure, with a torrent of Italianate English, was something to remember, if only for its rarity. I find it extraordinarily difficult to guess his contribution. As a critic it was undeniably very considerable indeed. As an eliminator of mistakes and red-herrings and as a puncturer of other people's over-inflated bright ideas it was immense. I do not myself remember him as a major provider himself of bright new ideas. But that element in a collective operation may easily be overvalued. And of Piero Sraffa's creativity in everything that he himself set out to tackle there can be no possible question.[37]

Meanwhile Sraffa's own work continued. By that time he was undoubtedly an expert in monetary theory; on 22 September 1931, for instance, he read a paper entitled 'Un économiste mathématicien du XVIIIème siècle: le général Lloyd' at a meeting of the first congress of the Econometric Society, organized by the University of Lausanne.[38]

It is far from easy, however, to evaluate the influence of Marx on Sraffa at this point. The Cambridge archives may very well disclose some interesting information about these links in the years to come. According to reliable accounts, Sraffa had acquired, in the early thirties, a reputation as an 'authority' on Marx's economic theory. A Keynes student, Tarshis recalled that Sraffa 'had a great reputation, at least among the students, as a Marx scholar';[39] Austin Robinson, talking about the 'Circus' of 1931, said: 'Piero Sraffa, of course, was the best Marxian scholar among us.'[40] Undoubtedly this opinion has to be considered with caution, because Marx's work was at that time largely unknown among Cambridge economists. Although very active as a militant, Dobb was not then known as a Marx scholar; nor was Joan Robinson .

In the summer of 1932, Keynes started work on his *General Theory of Employment, Interest and Money*. Between 1933 and 1935, Sraffa read some of the drafts of the book and made a series of criticisms, which did not always convince Keynes.[41] On 3 December 1933, for instance, Keynes wrote this to his wife:

> Piero of course made some exhausting difficulties, but nothing of real consequence, I am glad to say.[42]

In another letter to her (18 June 1934), he mentioned a lively discussion which had lasted six hours, interrupted by dinner with Piero's parents.[43] Thus Sraffa appears to have participated actively in the discussion of the successive drafts of the *General Theory*, as he had previously done for the *Treatise on Money*. Here again, it is difficult to evaluate exactly what his opinion was of the content of Keynes's new book.[44] Again it was said that he was sceptical about the originality of the book's theories. It is certain that he spent much time discussing the monetary aspects of it with his friend Dennis H. Robertson, who in his works expressed his particular thanks to him on two separate occasions.[45]

THE DISPUTE ABOUT MONEY WITH FRIEDRICH VON HAYEK

In January 1931, Friedrich August von Hayek (born 1899), Director of the Österreichisches Institut für Konjunkturforschung (Austrian Institute of Research on Business Cycles), and a lecturer at the University of Vienna, was asked by Lionel Robbins to read four papers at the London School of Economics. The papers were published two months later, under the title *Prices and Production*. Hayek was then offered a professorship at the London School of Economics by the Director, William Beveridge, and immediately opened hostilities with Keynes by attacking the *Treatise on Money* in the August issue of *Economica*.[46] He blamed Keynes for his obscurities and his confusing terminology and he criticized the author's conception, including profit, capital and investment. Keynes replied in the November issue of the same journal, accusing Hayek of not having understood his conclusions, though he admitted he had not propounded 'any satisfactory theory of capital and interest'. He said about *Prices and Production* that:

> The book, as it stands, seems to me to be one of the most frightful muddles I have ever read ... It is an extraordinary example of how, starting with a mistake, a remorseless logician can end up in Bedlam.[47]

The polemic continued with exchanges of letters between the two economists. Finally, Keynes asked Sraffa to write a critical review of *Prices and Production* for the *Economic Journal*. Sraffa agreed, and his piece 'Dr Hayek on Money and Capital'[48] came out in the March 1932 issue. Examining the arguments of Hayek's book, he argued that the characteristics of 'monetary economics' were being deliberately neglected; money appeared as a simple 'medium of exchange'. In reality, for Sraffa:

> money is not only the medium of exchange, but also a store of value, and the standard in terms of which debts, and other legal obligations, habits, opinions, conventions, in short all kinds of relations between men, are more or less rigidly fixed.[49]

Sraffa first emphasized the incongruities of the theory of 'forced saving' and then focused his critical attention on the 'relation of money to the rate of interest', which Hayek had developed from Wicksell. On this occasion, Sraffa introduced the concept of rate of interest that was taken up and developed by Keynes in chapter 17 of his *General Theory*.[50] Hayek replied in the June issue of the *Economic Journal*,[51] accusing Sraffa of not having understood anything about the theory he had developed in *Prices and Production*, or even about the theory of the *Treatise on Money*! Keynes reacted curtly to this accusation and added a note at the end of Hayek's reply:

> With Prof. Hayek's permission I should like to say that, to the best of my comprehension, Mr. Sraffa has understood my theory accurately.[52]

Sraffa commented again in the same issue of the *Economic Journal*, on a few specific points, while refusing to revise his overall opinion of the book.[53]

Life in Cambridge and the new friends he had made did not lead Sraffa to forget his anti-fascist compatriots. In the previous chapter we saw how active he was in helping Gramsci, and the contacts he had with the leaders of the Italian Communist Party exiled in France. Therefore, we will now examine some of the discussions and relationships he had with friends who were all, in their different ways, fighting Mussolini's regime.

In 1927, Sraffa began a correspondence with Tasca, who lived in Paris, editing the theoretical review *Lo Stato Operaio*. Their main concern was Gramsci's defence, but they also discussed two other interesting but very different issues: the significance of the Fascist economic policy of revaluing the lira in 1926–27, and the preparation of a critical edition of the letters of the first Italian Marxist philosopher, Antonio Labriola, to Friedrich Engels.

THE DISPUTE WITH ANGELO TASCA ABOUT THE REVALUATION OF THE LIRA

After the 'battle for grain' and the 'battle for population' (1925), Mussolini had announced on 18 August 1926 the 'battle for the lira' in a famous speech at Pesaro. During the following months, the regime inaugurated a stringent policy of revaluation of the lira, in flagrant opposition to the general opinion of the Italian monetary specialists. In August 1926, the pound sterling was worth 150 lire; in July 1927, it was worth about 90 lire and was soon stabilized at that price, the famous 'quota novanta'. The policy of deflation led to a recession in 1927, and accentuated the effect of the world economic crisis in 1929–30, especially for the banks. In August 1927, Tasca criticized this policy in the article 'La rivalutazione della lira e la crisi della economia italiana', published in *Lo Stato Operaio*. Nevertheless, he admitted that:

> any bourgeois government in power in Italy would have been confronted with the problem of monetary stabilization ..., consequently, there is no contradiction between the 'Fascist' policy of deflation and the policy dictated by the fundamental interests of the bourgeoisie.[54]

Sraffa read this analysis, and, when he passed through Paris at the beginning of September, briefly expressed his disagreement to the author, but the latter misunderstood the criticisms. Sraffa then explained his arguments in a letter of 17 September 1927:

> In general, it seems to me erroneous – and very dangerous – to believe that any isolated act of the Fascist government (or of any capitalist government) should be *directly* dictated by the *immediate* interests of the banks and the main industrialists. In applying this very simple and slightly naive principle, you are nevertheless obliged to deny that Fascism, during the last year, has deliberately produced deflation .... Mussolini wanted to revalue, even more than he has, but slowly: however, a slow revaluation is impossible.

Further on he added:

> My explanation is that, as I have already told you, this revaluation (besides being due to considerations of prestige and similar stupidities), is part of an attempt by Fascism to obtain the support of the middle class and some strata of the working class – since it cannot be denied that the only people who really benefit from the revaluation are to be found in those classes. And it is also evidently in the interest (non-immediate, 'obviously') of high finance that the State should consolidate its bases – even at the price of a few billions – by drawing towards itself the support of those strata which had been the support of the previous regime and which had, up to

> now and for a long time past, left Fascism and its bosses in a dangerous situation of isolation.[55]

Sraffa's position is very interesting, particularly when linked with the position defended a few years later by Togliatti. Indeed, the latter admitted, in his *Lezioni sul fascismo*, that the Italian Communist Party had, before and after 1922, committed serious errors of judgment regarding the 'petty bourgeoisie'.[56]

But Tasca remained certain that his analysis was well founded. He replied, in a letter of 2 October, that he was convinced that not every action of the Fascist government could be taken as having been dictated by the 'immediate' interests of the 'grande bourgeoisie'. However, he did not think that Fascism was trying to gain the support of the middle class; first it had to survive the monetary crisis, an indispensable condition if it was hold on to power and to continue to look after the interests of the bourgeoisie; it was in this light that the operation of 'stabilization' of the lira should be understood.[57] Sraffa expressed his disagreement in another letter, dated 15 October 1927. He criticized his friend for ignoring the crucial distinction between 'revaluation' and 'stabilization' of a currency. In 1926, according to him, 'the real and present conflict between class interests was in the choice between stabilization and revaluation'.[58] A reply of 21 October showed that the Communist leader had not been very impressed by the arguments propounded by the economist:

> First of all, is it true that revaluation always favours the middle class and 'a few strata of the working class'? This assertion belongs to the realm of generic truths, which are of little use when one examines the real consequences of a given monetary policy and its repercussions on the various classes.[59]

But it is also true that Tasca was very keen to pursue the dialogue and, some time later, he suggested to Sraffa that certain extracts should be published in *Lo Stato Operaio*.[60] Sraffa agreed,[61] and the correspondence was published in the November–December issue of the review, under the title 'Polemica monetaria'.[62]

Later, Sraffa and Tasca exchanged views on the 1930 Italian economic crisis, especially on its banking aspects.[63] Sraffa sent some information to his friend, including some material from the Banca Commerciale Italiana, where Mattioli worked.

SRAFFA'S ASSISTANCE TO TASCA IN EDITING LABRIOLA'S LETTERS TO ENGELS

The second subject of discussion in the Sraffa-Tasca correspondence was the letters written by the Neapolitan philosopher Labriola to Engels, between April 1880 and May 1895. In September 1927, Tasca started work on a complete edition of the letters sent to Engels by Labriola, using copies given to him by David Riazanov, Director of the Marx-Engels Institute in Moscow.[64] Tasca was preparing a weighty critical apparatus of footnotes, which demanded an enormous amount of work, and which unfortunately has no equivalent among recent Italian publications. In September 1927 Tasca, who could not go to Italy without risking arrest and a heavy sentence, asked Sraffa to lend him the three essays by Labriola on the 'materialist conception of history':[65] *In memoria del Manifesto dei Comunisti*,[66] *Del materialismo storico*,[67] and *Discorrendo di socialismo e di filosofia*.[68] Sraffa, who had these works in his library in Milan, agreed, and asked his father to send them to him in Cambridge. In October they were conveyed to Tasca,[69] who indicated not long afterwards that he had conceived of a 'vague project' on 'Labriola's philosophical thought'.[70] The first group of letters was published in *Lo Stato Operaio* as early as September 1927, and others appeared at intervals up to February 1930, making a total of 131 letters sent by Labriola to Engels.[71]

Tasca asked Sraffa whether he could do some research to help him finalize the notes to two of the letters: those of 28 October 1892 and 16 August 1894.[72] For the first letter, he wanted information about a Trades Union Congress of 1892 and about an article quoted by Labriola, which had been written by Edward Aveling and published the same year in the *Pall Mall Gazette*. For the second letter, Tasca needed some information about a review exaggeratedly praising Loria, written by James Bonar and published in the *Economic Journal* in March 1894,[73] and which was quoted by Labriola. Sraffa did his research at the British Museum Library, and sent on the necessary information.[74] Below are Tasca's notes for Labriola's two letters, published in *Lo Stato Operaio*, where Sraffa's help was most important; they follow the information given by the latter very closely.

For the first letter, of 28 October 1892, Tasca wrote that:

> The article to which Labriola here alludes came out in the *Pall Mall Gazette* of 11 October 1892, with the title 'Discord in the "International": Continental Opinion on the British Trade Unionists'. In it Aveling examined the attitude of the workers and socialist organizations of continental Europe towards the request made by the 25 Trades Union Congress (held in Candleriggs, Glasgow, from 5 to 10 October 1892) to convene an International Congress on the eight-hour working day.[75]

Discussing the second letter, of 16 August 1894, he mentioned that:

> Bonar, historian of economic doctrines, and scientifically much more serious than Loria, reviewed *Les Bases économiques de la constitution sociale*, published in Paris a year before, in the quoted issue of the *Economic Journal* [Vol. 11, March 1894] (pp. 76–82). By and large, Bonar does not accept Loria's theories, and still less those of Marx. He ends his article by praising Loria: 'It may be doubted if any other economist of our time has written so much to interest and stimulate; and there was probably never, even in Germany, one so thoroughly conversant with the literature of his subject in almost every European language.'[76]

What was Sraffa's reaction when he read Tasca's editing work? It can only be deduced from a letter he wrote to Tasca on 24 February 1928:

> Labriola's letters seem to me to be fairly insipid, at least the ones you have so far published. (In your introductory note, in fascicle 7, I see that you did not mention the two articles with bibliography which Croce published on Labriola in the *Critica* about twenty years ago: they were part of a 'series'; I cannot remember whether it was of famous historiographers or famous Italians.)[77]

It seems that Sraffa was referring here to two articles by Croce, published in *La Critica: Rivista di letteratura, storia e filosofia*, in 1907 and 1909 respectively.[78] The publication of the (almost complete) edition of Labriola's letters to Engels ended in February 1930. Tasca had by then already broken with the Italian Communist Party, and Sraffa does not seem to have had any further contact with him after this date.

FRIENDSHIP WITH ITALIAN ANTI-FASCISTS: MATTIOLI AND MORANDI

At the beginning of the thirties, Sraffa was also in touch with some non-communist anti-fascist friends who had remained in Italy, notably Raffaele Mattioli and Rodolfo Morandi.

In 1931 Mattioli, whose role in preserving Gramsci's *Prison Notebooks* in 1937–38 has already been touched upon, became chief executive of the Banca Commerciale Italiana. He joined the National Fascist Party, though he was in fact anti-fascist. He wrote the celebrated essay, 'Per la regolamentazione dell' economia Italiana', which was given to Benito Mussolini by Giuseppe Toeplitz, managing director of the bank, in September 1931. This essay recommended that the Fascist economy, weakened by the crisis, should change into an 'economia regolata', thus opening the way to state control over the credit institutions. In 1933, the Istituto per la Ricostruzione Industriale (IRI) was set up; the Banca Commerciale Italiana formally became part of the IRI, as did the Credito Mobiliare and the Banco di Roma. Mattioli was promoted to the post of Managing Director of the Banca Commerciale Italiana, a position which he held until 1960.[79] He was a friend of the 'neo-idealist' philosopher Croce, and had become highly cultured, a passionate book collector, especially of seventeenth and eighteenth century books. Sraffa made use of his scholarship when he was preparing the collected edition of David Ricardo's writings.[80] Being well acquainted with the work of Keynes, Mattioli was also responsible for having the *Treatise on Money* translated into Italian so rapidly.[81]

Sraffa may have known Morandi (1902–55) through Carlo Rosselli. Born in Milan, Morandi went to Pavia in 1921 to study law, and obtained his doctorate from the University of Milan in 1925. He was an active anti-fascist, and a contributor to Piero Gobetti's *Rivoluzione Liberale*, and to Carlo Rosselli and Pietro Nenni's *Il Quarto Stato*. In 1927, following the advice of his friend Lelio Basso, he went to Germany to study Marxism, and took an interest in economics. In 1928–29, he wrote the important essay *Storia della grande industria in Italia*, published by Laterza in 1931.[82] Some time in 1929 or 1931, he became a member of the underground organization Giustizia e Libertà, and afterwards played an active role in the Italian Socialist Party, advocating cooperation between the Socialists and the Communists; in 1934, he launched the Centro Interno Socialista.

Around 1931–32, Morandi had the idea of starting a series of books with the aim of creating a centre of cultural opposition to Fascism. In particular, he wanted to publish a series of complete texts of the 'classics' of economics, from Adam Smith to Marx, 'somewhat similar to Laterza's philosophy series' – a reference to the 'Classics of Modern Philosophy', edited, from 1906 on, by Benedetto Croce and Giovanni Gentile. A second series of works on non-classical economics was also to be launched, including J. A. Hobson, Max Weber, Werner Sombart, etc. In the spring of 1932 Morandi consulted Sraffa to work out a list of works for these two series, and asked him to be a member of the team that would be in charge of preparing the editions.[83] But the project never came to anything owing to problems over money. At the beginning of 1933, Morandi became an editor at the Corticelli publishing house in Milan; he tried to revive the project of a series of 'classics' of political economy (Turgot, Smith, Ricardo, etc.), and asked his friend which of the original editions should be used. In his answer, in February or early March 1934, Sraffa mentioned the Cannan edition[84] of *The Wealth of Nations* by Adam Smith, and his own edition of Ricardo's *Principles of Political Economy and Taxation*, to be published in the Collected Works, announced for the autumn.[85] This second attempt was also unsuccessful. In April 1937,

Morandi was arrested and sentenced to ten years in prison for having launched a subversive organization; he remained in prison until 1943.[86]

THE SECOND WORLD WAR

In May 1940, the 'phoney war' on the western front ended when the Germans invaded France and started their relentless bombing of England. The British government, faced with the activities of the Axis countries, decided on the immediate arrest of all Italian and German citizens. Sraffa, who held an Italian passport, was arrested in Cambridge, and taken to an internment camp on the Isle of Man, where he met some anti-Nazi German intellectuals, including H. W. Singer, Edward Rosenbaum (who had been Director of the Commerzbibliothek of Hamburg), and Erwin Rothbarth, who had helped Keynes prepare the brochure *How to Pay for the War* (1940). His stay was supposed to be temporary, as the British government was thinking of transferring the prisoners to a concentration camp in the Dominions as soon as possible. In July, Keynes and his mother, Florence Ada Keynes, Mayor of Cambridge since 1932, used their influence in high places to free Sraffa.[87] As Charles H. Hession stated, Sraffa wrote to Keynes from the camp, 'thanking him for everything he was doing and asking whether his [Keynes's] mother could comfort his own mother, who was at the time alone and without friends in Cambridge'.[88] Keynes's efforts proved successful, and Sraffa was able to return to Cambridge University at the end of the summer, and to pursue his research.

Among Cambridge economists, a new 'circle' was coming into being in 1940: its members included Kahn and Kaldor as well as Sraffa. It was named the 'war circus', and went on until 1965, as the 'secret seminar': and indeed, only a lucky few were ever invited to participate in the meetings.[89]

At the beginning of the Second World War, the Economics Faculty of the LSE was evacuated to Cambridge. Pigou decided to organize a cycle of conferences on the 'great economists'. Kaldor, who recorded this episode, indicates that the choice of speakers and subjects was: Charles Ryle Fay on Adam Smith, Piero Sraffa on David Ricardo, Gerald Shove on John Stuart Mill, Maurice Dobb on Karl Marx, Joan Robinson on William Stanley Jevons and Claude W. Guillebaud on Alfred Marshall. The day before he was due to speak, Sraffa went to see Pigou and asked him whether he could not be exempted from reading his paper, explaining that a 'psychological block' prevented him from appearing in public. He was called upon to find a replacement quickly, and his choice was Nicholas Kaldor.[90]

During his first years in Cambridge Sraffa prepared himself for his major work – the editing of Ricardo's writings and the publication of the brief essay, *Production of Commodities by Means of Commodities* – as we shall now find out.

4 The publication of Ricardo's *Collected Works* and of *Production of Commodities by Means of Commodities*: extensive research

INITIAL RESEARCH FOR *PRODUCTION OF COMMODITIES BY MEANS OF COMMODITIES*

During his first years in Cambridge, Piero Sraffa had initiated the research which led, much later, to the publication of his famous essay *Production of Commodities by Means of Commodities: Prelude to a Critique of Economic Theory*. In 1926, in 'The Laws of Returns under Competitive Conditions', he had already maintained that the classical economists' theory of value, and the problems it raised, met with total 'indifference' among contemporary economists, most of whom were faithful to the marginal approach. But Sraffa, even though he himself had pioneered the idea of imperfect competition, had soon lost confidence in its prospects, and was showing increasing interest in the problems raised by the theory of value and distribution as defined by Smith, Ricardo and Marx; he was also interested in the approach of the physiocrat François Quesnay, who had been the first to consider production and consumption as a 'circular process'. Sraffa attempted to rehabilitate and reformulate the theoretical approach based on the notion of 'surplus', as a potential starting point for a radical critique of the marginal approach to capital and distribution, based on the notion of 'factors of production'.

An important part of his research concerned Ricardo. Ricardo accepted the principle of labour-embodied value, but introduced a number of deviations and exceptions, for example greater or lesser machine durability, and different combinations of fixed and circulating capital. Furthermore, he was looking for an 'invariable measure of value', a standard independent of changes in the distribution of income between wages and profits, but also independent of variations in commodity production techniques. Not long after his arrival at King's College, Sraffa discussed his research with Keynes, who gave the following assessment to his wife Lydia:

On Saturday I had a long talk with Sraffa about his work. It is very

> interesting and *original* – but I wonder whether his class will understand him when he lectures.[1]

In 1928, Sraffa asked Keynes to read a 'draft of the opening propositions' treated in his study. As Sraffa's drafts are still unpublished, it is impossible at the moment to give details about these and subsequent drafts. Nevertheless, it would appear that Sraffa had been inspired by the reproduction schemes in Volume 2 of Marx's *Capital*. Keynes showed interest in the work, and 'recommended that, if constant returns were *not* to be assumed, an emphatic warning to the effect should be given' to the reader.[2] In exchange, as we have already seen, Keynes asked Sraffa to read various drafts of his *Treatise on Money*.

By the close of the twenties, the 'central propositions' of the developing work were already in place. Some of Sraffa's research had a mathematical dimension and, for a short while, in 1928 and 1929, he was able to make use of the advice of his friend Ramsey, who died prematurely in January 1930, after which Sraffa's sources of technical advice were two mathematicians from Cambridge University – first, Alister Watson, and later A. S. Besicovitch.[3] Between the years 1932 and 1940, Sraffa developed some of the distinctive points of his theory, for example the introduction of 'fixed capital' and 'joint production', into his systems of equations; and he finally succeeded in building a 'standard commodity', that is to say, a standard independent of changes in the distribution of 'surplus' between wages and profits, for a given production method.

LAYING THE FOUNDATIONS OF THE DEFINITIVE EDITION OF RICARDO'S COLLECTED WORKS

In 1930, while doing research on *Production of Commodities by Means of Commodities*, Sraffa started work on his scholarly edition of Ricardo's *Collected Works*, which was to include not only all his works, manuscripts and articles, but also his entire economic correspondence.

One of Ricardo's disciples, John Ramsay McCulloch, had already done some work in collecting the writings and had published *The Works of David Ricardo*.[4] From the late nineteenth century onwards, various other works were published. In 1887 James Bonar published Ricardo's letters to Malthus (1810–23), and later, in 1899, helped by Jacob H. Hollander, Ricardo's letters to Hutches Trower and other correspondents (1811–23). In 1895 Hollander published Ricardo's letters to McCulloch (1816–23). After additional archives had been brought to light by Colonel Frank Ricardo in 1919, Hollander and T. E. Gregory published the *Notes on Malthus's Principles of Political Economy*, but not until 1928. In 1931 Hollander published McCulloch's letters to Ricardo (1818–23); then, in 1932, the *Minor Papers on the Currency System* (1809–23).

In 1925 the Royal Economic Society launched a project to publish Ricardo's collected works and entrusted the task to T. E. Gregory, of the London School of Economics, who did not, however, get very far with it. Around March 1930, Keynes, secretary of the Royal Economic Society since 1923, managed to convince the new president, Herbert Somerton Foxwell, that if Gregory would agree, the task should be handed over to Sraffa. An announcement appeared in the *Economic Journal* in December, indicating that this 'definitive and complete edition' of the works of Ricardo would probably consist of seven volumes.[5] In 1931 Gramsci, in his prison cell, learned about the project after reading Einaudi's article 'Per una nuova collana di economisti' in *La Riforma Sociale*.[6] He declared himself very pleased with the news, and added:

> I hope I shall be in a position to read English with ease when this edition comes out, and so be able to read Ricardo in the original.[7]

Gramsci would have liked to use *On the Principles of Political Economy and Taxation* for his research, but was unable to obtain it, although an Italian translation had been published in the Biblioteca dell' Economista series (1856), and reprinted in 1925 with an introduction by Achille Loria.[8] He had to content himself with the critical presentation by Charles Gide, in the well-known manual written with the help of Charles Rist, *Histoire des doctrines économiques depuis les physiocrates jusqu'à nos jours*.[9]

Sraffa sent his answer a month later, via Tatiana Schucht:

> When you write to Nino, tell him that what he said about the edition of the works of Ricardo, which I am preparing, made me very happy; I hope it will come out here in a year and a half or two years, and I will of course send him a copy.[10]

Sraffa immediately got down to the task. In a letter dated 22 March 1930, he sought advice from Keynes as to whom he should contact, and informed him that he had just spent 'five days working' with Dobb, Kahn and K. S. Isles, comparing the different versions of Ricardo's *On the Principles of Political Economy and Taxation*.[11] He meant to publish not only all Ricardo's letters but also all those of his correspondents, and started looking for unpublished letters, especially among Ricardo's descendants and inheritors; Keynes took an active part in this search. Sraffa got in touch with David Ricardo's great-grandsons, Lieutenant Colonel Henry George Ricardo[12] and Colonel Frank Ricardo.[13] He also met Robert Malthus, descendant of the famous curate. The year 1930 was particularly rich in discoveries. At the beginning of April, Colonel Frank Ricardo informed the Royal Economic Society that a great quantity of letters had been found at Bromesberrow Place, near Ledbury, which had been the residence of Osman, Ricardo's eldest son. We know through Keynes how Sraffa reacted when at last he had the chance to consult the documents:

> Piero was at a pitch of excitement and stayed up all night, until six o'clock next morning, reading them.[14]

On 5 June, Sraffa wrote in a letter to his former teacher, Luigi Einaudi:

> We have managed to unearth (it is still a secret for the moment) a good many letters of Malthus, McCulloch, Bentham, Trower, and what is even more exciting, about forty-five letters by James Mill; not counting half a dozen important letters by R[icardo], of which he had kept a copy. And I am on the track of more, I hope.

In the same letter, Sraffa exposed his deep regret at the lack of success of his search, in France, for Ricardo's letters to Jean-Baptiste Say. Sraffa had written to André Liesse, a good friend of Léon Say, but without success.[15] In 1932, he found traces of these letters in Le Havre, in the possession of a great-grandson of Jean-Baptiste Say, Edgar Raoul-Duval.[16] At the end of 1930, Colonel Frank Ricardo also discovered a new batch of letters from various correspondents of Ricardo's,[17] which was a further source of pleasure to Sraffa.

While editing the texts and letters of Ricardo, Sraffa took advice from Keynes, James Bonar, Edwin Cannan, Theodore E. Gregory and from Luigi Einaudi in Italy, who, in a 1936 study, 'Come non si devono ristampare i nostri classici', set down some technical criteria for editing the 'classics' of political economy.[18]

By 1930, Sraffa was already establishing his reputation as an expert on Ricardo. He reacted vigorously to an essay by Einaudi, published in November 1929 in the *Quarterly Journal of Economics*, entitled 'James Pennington or James Mill: an early Correction of Ricardo', which attributed to Ricardo a miscalculation in his presentation of the law of comparative costs. In a note dealing mainly with philological matters, 'An Alleged Correction of Ricardo', published in the same journal in May 1930, Sraffa attempted to prove that this 'miscalculation' had in fact been committed by James Mill, and had been wrongly attributed to Ricardo by John Stuart Mill, probably to spare his father's reputation. Einaudi, whose reply was published immediately after Sraffa's note, gracefully admitted his mistake.[19]

Between 1931 and 1933, within the framework of his work as editor, Sraffa began some research on Ricardo's life, in which he was assisted by the descendants of the economist, particularly Colonel Frank Ricardo, who put numerous documents at his disposal, as well as the few books left from

Ricardo's personal library. In 1932, Sraffa asked for research to be done in the archives of the Jewish community of Livorno about the origin of Ricardo's family.[20] He also travelled to Holland to examine some parochial registers and clergyman's memoirs, and to try and make clearer Ricardo's attitude to religion, especially with regard to his brief adherence to the Unitarian Chapel. He contacted the banking houses of Lombard Street in London concerning Ricardo's financial activities. In the autumn of 1933, when Sraffa was in Paris, Huguette Biaujeaud, a French student, presented to him her research on Ricardo's theory of value, which had already reached an advanced stage. Sraffa sent her, among other things, unpublished details about Ricardo's life[21] which he had gathered for future use in the *Biographical Miscellany*, Volume X of the *Collected Works*.[22]

Sraffa did not expect that his editorial work would take him long. As we have seen, in 1931 he had told Gramsci that the books would be published between March and October 1933. For his part, Keynes also said that the work of Sraffa 'from whom nothing is hid', would come out in 1933,[23] but the promised publication did not take place. In spring 1934, Sraffa was certain it would appear in the autumn,[24] but after 1934 made no further mention of imminent publication. The difficulties encountered in preparing the publication of the texts as well as the correspondence were greater than had been expected. Moreover, scholarly scruples prompted him to pursue his search for the lost letters.

AN IMPORTANT EXCHANGE OF VIEWS WITH GRAMSCI ABOUT THE PHILOSOPHICAL IMPLICATIONS OF RICARDO'S THEORY

Two years after Sraffa had started work on the edition of the collected works, a series of discussions took place between Sraffa and Gramsci about Ricardo's theory. In a letter of 30 May 1932, addressed to Tatiana Schucht, Gramsci sought advice from his friend about Ricardo's importance in the development of historical materialism:

> I'd like now to tell you about one or two points I've been turning over in my head, so that if you think it's worth it you can copy them out for Piero, and ask him to supply a few references about books which will help me to enlarge the field of my cogitations and get myself better orientated. What I would like to know is this: does any special work exist (maybe in English?) on Ricardo's methods of research into economics, and on the innovations which Ricardo introduced into critical methodology? I should imagine that on the centenary of his death, ten years ago,[25] a valuable literature on this subject may well have appeared, and that it might be

quite possible to find something which exactly suited the research I am engaged on just now.

The train of my thought is more or less as follows: can one maintain that Ricardo has an importance in the history of philosophy, as distinct from the history of economics, in which he is certainly a figure of the first order? And can one say that Ricardo helped to put the first theorists of the philosophy of *praxis* on the road which led to their overcoming the Hegelian philosophy and constructing a new historicism, freed from every trace of speculative logic? It seems to me that one could make an attempt to prove the truth of these assertions, and that it would be worthwhile undertaking this. I would base myself on the two fundamental concepts of economics, 'determinate market' ('mercato determinato')[26] and 'law as a statement of tendency' ('legge di tendence'), which I believe we owe to Ricardo, and proceed as follows: it is not possible that these two concepts served as a starting-point when the attempt was being made to reduce the 'immanentist' conception of history (expressed as it was in the idealistic and speculative language of classical German philosophy) to a realistic, immediately historical 'immanence' – an 'immanence' in which the law of causality of the natural sciences had been purged of its mechanistic character, and left free to identify itself systematically with the dialectical reasoning of Hegelianism?

Perhaps this whole nexus of ideas is still a bit fuzzy and opaque, but it's important that it should be comprehended as a whole, even if only approximately: sufficiently, at any rate, for Piero to be able to tell me whether this problem has ever been perceived or tackled by any student of Ricardo.

It is opportune to remember that Hegel himself, in other cases, was aware of these necessary nexi between diverse scientific activities – and also between scientific and political activities. Thus in his *Lectures on the History of Philosophy* he discovered a nexus between the French Revolution and the philosophy of Kant, Fichte and Schelling, and said that 'only two people, the French and the German, although the opposite of each other in so many ways (maybe, indeed, *because* they are such opposites) took part in the great epoch of universal history at the end of the eighteenth century and the beginning of the nineteenth, the reason being that while in Germany the new principle burst forth as *spirit* and *concept*, in France it took shape as effective reality'. If you look up *The Holy Family* you will see that the theorists of the philosophy of *praxis* established this very nexus between French political activity and the above-mentioned German philosophy. What I want to find out is how much classical English economic theory (in the methodological form elaborated by Ricardo) contributed to the further development of the new theory, and in what manner it exerted this influence.

That the classical English economic theory contributed to the development of the new philosophy is commonly admitted, but usually one thinks merely of Ricardo's theory of value. It seems to me that we must look a little further and identify a contribution which I would call synthetic (that is, bound up with the intuition of the world and the manner of thinking) and not merely analytical (in relation to a particular doctrine, however fundamental). P., in the course of his work on the critical edition of the works of Ricardo, might collect a lot of valuable material relating to the whole question. Anyway, I'd be grateful if he could find out whether any book dealing with the subject does exist, and thus be of real help to me in my present condition as a prisoner – that is, while I am unable to do systematic research in libraries myself.[27]

Gramsci wanted more precise information about Ricardo's methodology. He thought that the deductive method ('if we suppose that ...') had led Ricardo not to the construction of abstract generalities, but to the examination of a determined 'social form', and thus to bring to light the 'determinate market', that is to say, a set of specific economic activities implying the existence of a certain balance of power between social classes,[28] every class acting according to a specific 'rationality'. On this foundation, according to Gramsci, Ricardo established 'laws as a statement of tendency', which were laws not in the sense given to them by naturalism or speculative determinism, but in the 'historicist' sense, in so far as a 'determinate market', exists.[29] Yet the crux of the problem was the position of Ricardo in the background of Marx: was Ricardo an innovator from the gnoseological and philosophical point of view and, as such, was his role in the passage from Hegelianism to Marxism that of a catalyst?

On 21 June, Sraffa conveyed his answer in a letter to Tatiana Schucht, who copied it word for word in a letter to Gramsci, dated 5 July:

Nino can guess how interesting I found his observations. As to the main one, concerning Ricardo's significance for the history of philosophy, I will have to think about it – and to understand it fully, I will have to go much further in my studies than the writings of Ricardo, to those of the first theorists of the philosophy of praxis. I would nevertheless like more in the way of explanation about the two concepts of a 'determinate market' and 'law as a statement of tendency', which are said by Nino to be fundamental, and to which, by putting them in quotation, he seems to be giving a technical meaning: I admit that I do not understand very well what they refer to, and as regards the second, I have been used to considering it more as one of the characteristics of vulgar economics. It

> is in any case very difficult to evaluate the philosophical importance, if any, of Ricardo's thinking, since, unlike the philosophers of praxis, he never subjected his own thinking to historical considerations. He rarely placed himself in a historical perspective and, as has been said, he considered the laws of the society in which he lived to be natural and immutable.[30]

It is interesting to note that Sraffa saw the concept of 'law as a statement of tendency' as a contribution, not by Ricardo, but by 'vulgar economics'. The reference is to Marshall's *Principles of Economics*,[31] which defined law as 'statement of tendency'. He refused, rightly, to consider Ricardo as a 'historicist' thinker, and in general remained sceptical about his importance from a philosophical point of view. About this, he noted in the letter that 'the only cultural element to be found there is derived from the natural sciences'.[32] For the time being, Sraffa believed, he could not give his friend any decisive information; nevertheless he sent him a number of bibliographical references, one of which is especially interesting: a collection of Marx's early writings, published in Germany by Siegfried Landhut and J. P. Mayer, *Der historische Materialismus. Die Frühschriften*.[33] The first volume contains the *Kritik der Hegelschen Staatsrecht*, which had already been published in German in 1927,[34] and an unpublished text, the famous 'Ökonomisch-philosophische Manuscripte aus dem Jahre 1844'.[35] Sraffa was convinced that this latter was of paramount importance for the clarification of the problem posed by his friend.

Unfortunately it is not known whether Gramsci ever received the letter; and the dialogue, although very promising, was never followed up.

THE PUBLICATION OF RICARDO'S COLLECTED WORKS

During the second half of the thirties, research on the edition of Ricardo's collected works progressed slowly. From 1936 to 1939, Sraffa was assisted by Mrs A. Barbara Lowe.[36] In the spring of 1940, six volumes were ready to be printed, but the introductions had not yet been written, and the Second World War forced Sraffa to postpone the project. Fifty years later, we can see how fortunate this postponement was. In June 1943 Charles King Mill, a relative of John Stuart Mill, found an important set of documents at Raheny, near Dublin, in the castle of his father-in-law, F. E. Cairnes (son of the economist John Elliot Cairnes), who had died not long before. The economist George O'Brien discovered among the documents some correspondence between John Elliot Cairnes and his friend John Stuart Mill.[37] Sraffa, who had been told about the discovery by Hayek, got in touch with C. K. Mill to find out whether there were any letters by Ricardo among the papers. On being told that there were, he went to Raheny, where he made an extraordinary discovery: a bundle with an inscription in James Mill's handwriting, 'Mr David Ricardo's Manuscripts'. The bundle contained a series of fifty-seven letters from Ricardo to James Mill, covering the period 1811 to 1823, but also some unknown manuscripts, such as the now famous essay 'Absolute Value and Exchangeable Value' (1823).

On 5 July, Sraffa sent a full-blown report of the discovery to Keynes, who was in Washington at the time.[38] These archives proved to be so rich in material that the original scheme of publication had to be revised entirely. After the end of the Second World War it was thought that the edition would consist of ten volumes, of which four would contain the correspondence and two others the pamphlets and papers. During the second half of 1947, Sraffa was helped (not very efficiently) by Miss Lucy Munby; at the beginning of 1948, Austin Robinson (Secretary of the Royal Economic Society), much worried about the delays in the appearance of the edition, asked Dobb, who was shortly to be elected to a fellowship and lectureship at Trinity College, to help Sraffa finish Ricardo's volumes. The two friends worked together between February 1948 and June 1954.[39] Dobb, who was generally free only during university holidays, helped to write the notes and introductions to Volumes I, II, V and VI.

Since the death of his mother in 1945, Sraffa had been living in rooms at Trinity College. In the summer of 1948, he decided to show post-war Italy to his Cambridge friends, Richard Kahn and Joan Robinson. The three of them enjoyed hiking in the mountains, and when they were not scaling the heights, they were immersing themselves in Roy Harrod's book *Towards a Dynamic Economics*, which came out shortly after.[40]

The first four volumes of Ricardo's collected works were brought to completion between 1949 and 1950, and were published the following year. The first volume, *On the Principles of Political Economy and Taxation*, contained a 'General Preface' and the important 'Introduction'. Concerning both these texts, Dobb remarked to Theodore Prager on 23 December 1950:

> In particular I think we conclusively establish (in opposition to the traditional Hollander–Marshall-Cannan view) that there was no 'weakening' of Ricardo's enunciation of the labour theory as time went on: that in fact he reached at the end of his life a position rather close to that of Marx, so that the true line of descent is certainly from Ricardo to Marx, and *not* from Ricardo to cost-of-production theory [and] Mill to Marshall as the bourgeois tradition has it.[41]

The second volume contained the *Notes on Malthus's Principles of Political Economy*. The *Pamphlets and Papers, 1809–1811* and *1815–1823*, made up Volumes III and IV. For that last volume Sraffa wrote in particular a 'Note on Fragments on Torrens' and a 'Note on Absolute Value and Exchangeable Value'.

Professor Luigi Einaudi, who was at the time the President of Italy,[42] wrote a review of the first two volumes for the *Giornale degli Economisti*, with the title 'Dalla leggenda al monumento'.[43] This review, in which he began by teasing his friend about the slow progress of his editing work, focused solely on the philological aspects. It totally ignored the originality of Sraffa's reading of Ricardo in the 'Introduction' to the first volume. Piero thanked his former teacher in a letter dated 6 September 1951, in which he took the liberty of pointing out a small mistake in the proofs of the review: Ricardo had not given evidence as a witness before the Bullion Committee, although he had certainly influenced it; he had appeared before the Committee on Usury Laws in 1818, and the two committees on Resumption of Cash Payment in 1819.[44]

1952 saw the publication of a large amount of material: Volume V, which contained *Speeches and Evidence*, and Volumes VI, VII, VIII and IX, which contained the entire correspondence, *Letters 1810–1815, 1816–1818, 1819–June 1821* and *July 1821–1823*, that is to say, 555 letters, of which 296 were by Ricardo and 259 by his correspondents: 317 of these were published for the first time. Nonetheless, Sraffa always regretted not having been able to find, for example, the letters from Ricardo to his friend, Pascoe Grenfell, who was a Member of Parliament and also sat on the Bullion Committee.

Volume X, the *Biographical Miscellany*, was finished in June 1954 and published in 1955. In the same year, Sraffa published a letter from Malthus to Ricardo dated c. January 1817, which was found in the Rothschild library, under the title 'Malthus on Public Works'.[45]

From this time on, Sraffa received numerous awards for his edition of Ricardo's works. In 1954, he became a Fellow of the British Academy; on 23 March 1961, in Stockholm, the King of Sweden, Gustav-Adolph, presented him with the Söderström gold medal of the Royal Academy of Sciences. This honorary distinction, which antedated the Nobel Prize for Economics, was also awarded to John Maynard Keynes and Gunnar Myrdal.

AN OUTSTANDING SCHOLAR OF THE HISTORY OF ECONOMIC THOUGHT

Frequent calls were made on Sraffa's prodigious scholarship in the history of economic thought, and more generally in the history of culture. Those who came to consult on one or other of a variety of problems were always received with the utmost courtesy and a helpfulness but also with reserve and tact. During the first years following the Second World War, he became an adviser to the publishing house founded in 1933 by Giulio Einaudi (born in 1911 in

Turin), who was one of the sons of Luigi Einaudi, Sraffa's former teacher. At the offices of the publishing house, he met some important associates of Giulio Einaudi, such as Antonio Giolitti and the 'Communist Catholic' Felice Balbo. In the autumn of 1948, Giulio told him that they were launching a series of 'classics' in economics, and asked his advice about an initial list of suitable authors. Sraffa replied in a letter dated 30 October 1948:

> About the series of economics classics: obviously such a series, if it is to be successful and of permanent value, should follow a consistent idea, like Ferrara's 'Biblioteca dell' Economista'. Up to now, no series of classical economists considered as sources of Marxism has ever been put together in any country, and such a series is long overdue. But it should be preceded by a decent edition of the works of Marx, especially of the *Theorien ü. den Mehrwert*, which gives some idea of the classical economists who should be included.
>
> I agree with the first names you mentioned. Nevertheless, neither Petty nor Quesnay (unlike A. Smith and Ricardo) is the author of a fundamental work as such – the *Tableau économique*, for example, is an opuscule of twenty to thirty pages. To the volumes you have indicated, I would unhesitatingly add Cantillon's *Essai sur la nature du commerce en général* (of which there is an Italian translation dating from the eighteenth century, though I do not know its value). This seems to me an excellent idea.[46]

At the start of this letter, Sraffa refers to the eighty-three volumes of the prestigious Biblioteca dell' Economista, published between 1850 and 1937.[47] But Sraffa felt that Cantillon's *Essai sur la nature du commerce en général* should be added to Einaudi's list. He had in his library the 1755 first edition, which his friend Mattioli had bought for a ridiculously low price from a reputable antique dealer, and had given him as present; this was recalled by Luigi Einaudi in a book dedicated to the history of economic thought.[48] Sraffa was alluding to the first Italian translation of the book, done by Scottoni and published in Venice in 1767. He agreed to be an adviser for Giulio Einaudi's series of Classici dell' Economia, which began in 1954 with the publication of the first volume of Karl Marx's *Theorien über den Mehrwert: Storia delle teorie economiche*, Volume 1, *La teoria del plusvalore da William Petty a Adam Smith*. The second volume, *David Ricardo*, and the third, *Da Ricardo all' economia volgare*, were published in 1955 and 1958, respectively. Only two other titles appeared in the series: Cantillon's *Saggi sulla natura del commercio in generale*, in a new translation, in 1955,[49] and Rosa Luxemburg's *Accumulazione del capitale* in 1960.

In 1958, Sraffa's scholarship was demonstrated in a long letter to Luigi Einaudi, following the publication in France of the anthology *François*

Quesnay et la Physiocratie,[50] to which his former teacher contributed with a 'Preface' and the article 'A propos de la date de publication de la Physiocratie'. On 22 August, Sraffa, to whom Mattioli had immediately sent the book, wrote to Luigi Einaudi, giving his impressions of the second volume, which contained the 'annotated texts'. In particular he remarked that the first appearance of the term 'Physiocratie' was not due to the Abbé Baudeau, in his weekly *Ephémérides du citoyen ou Chronique de l'esprit national*, in April 1767 – as was thought by August Oncken in 1886, and later by Georges Weulersse – but rather occurred in the announcement of the forthcoming publication of 'Physiocratie, ou Constitution naturelle du gouvernement le plus avantageux au genre humain', by Du Pont de Nemours, in the March 1767 issue of the same *Ephémérides*.[51] He also noted the enormous importance of Turgot's letter to Du Pont de Nemours dated 18 November 1767.

Part of Sraffa's duties as Assistant Director of Research consisted in supervising the work of some of the many students who had come to do research in Cambridge. Among those who benefited from his advice in the preparation of their doctoral theses were the New Zealander Ronald L. Meek (1917–78)[52] and the Australian Graham S. L. Tucker,[53] as well as the Italians Pierangelo Garegnani (born 1930)[54] and Luigi L. Pasinetti (born 1930).

Sraffa enjoyed the privilege of cordial relations with most of the important contemporary specialists in the history of economic thought. For example, he was in contact with the American William Jaffé, who spent many years preparing the monumental *Correspondence of Léon Walras and Related Papers*, which included a letter by Walras from Sraffa's own collection.[55]

THE COMPLETION OF *PRODUCTION OF COMMODITIES BY MEANS OF COMMODITIES*

From the middle of 1954, once he had finished work on his edition of Ricardo, Sraffa had a lot more free time. He participated in a study trip to the People's Republic of China, and wrote an article on the development of Anglo-Chinese trade between 1952 and 1955, for an Italian symposium on China.[56]

From January 1955 onwards, he once more began delving into his old research notes for *Production of Commodities by Means of Commodities*, a work he had more or less abandoned since the Second World War. He decided to order his material in chapters, with a new text, and to complete the treatment of some very important points, including for example, 'the adapting of the distinction between "basics" and "non-basics" to the case of joint products'.[57] He did not intend to publish the work immediately because he wanted to polish it further. But in 1957 he finished an overall draft while staying on the island of Majorca. Mattioli, soon to become chairman of the board of directors of the Banca Commerciale Italiana, persuaded him to proceed rapidly with publication both in Britain and in Italy. The author's numerous reservations were overcome one after another, and the preface was finally written in March 1959. Mattioli offered to help with the translation of the text into Italian. The work came out during the first months of 1960, first in Britain, as *Production of Commodities by Means of Commodities: Prelude to a Critique of Economic Theory*, and then in Italy, as *Produzione di merci a mezzo di merci: Premesse a una critica della teoria economica.*[58]

The writing of this book – hardly more than a hundred pages in the English edition – had required thirty-three years of gestation. It was divided into three parts – 'Single-product Industries and Circulating Capital', 'Multiple-product Industries and Fixed Capital' and 'Switch in Methods of Production' – and concluded with four appendices. In 1961–62 the book was reviewed in the major international economics reviews. The supporters of neo-classical orthodoxy questioned the originality of Sraffa's theoretical model or, at best, considered it as simply one more version of the input-output model of Wassily Leontieff, the Russian-born American economist.[59] The 'neo-Keynesian' economist Roy F. Harrod, in the review he wrote for the *Economic Journal*, greatly underestimated Sraffa's break with traditional theory, and maintained that 'peaceful coexistence' between the two was possible. According to him, the major characteristic of the book was the absence of any reference to consumer demand in the determination of 'prices of production'.[60] Harrod appeared not to have understood this point, as Sraffa replied in an article which was published in the *Economic Journal* in June 1962.[61]

In the *Revue suisse d'économie politique et de statistique*, Peter K. Newman thought it would be necessary to '*translate* his [Sraffa's] work into the more widely used Walrasian dialect of mathematical economics'.[62] Sraffa, in a letter to Newman (4 June 1962), commented on the review: he stated that, while disagreeing on the question of 'non-basic products', he was very interested in this 'transposition', with respect to the first part of the book.[63]

In the *Oxford Economic Papers*, Joan Robinson, a highly respected member of the 'Cambridge school', proposed an entirely different 'reading' of *Production of Commodities by Means of Commodities*: she placed special stress on the subtitle, *Prelude to a Critique of Economic Theory*, and identified three central assumptions from the 'corn-wage' model:

> The first is that, when we are provided with a set of technical equations for production and a real wage rate which is uniform throughout the

> economy, there is no room for demand equations in the determination of equilibrium prices ....
> The second proposition is mentioned by Sraffa in his *References to the Literature.* It is the rejection of the claim 'that the price of every commodity, either immediately or ultimately, resolves itself entirely (that is to say, without leaving any commodity residue) into wage, profit, and rent'...
> The third proposition, if we may indulge in a loose mode of expression that the author carefully avoids, is that the marginal productivity theory of distribution is all bosh.[64]

With reference to this third aspect it should be noted that, in the sixties, Sraffa's theses led to a debate about whether it was possible to quantify 'capital' without taking distribution into account, and to a further debate about the question of 'reswitching'. The Italian economist Claudio Napoleoni, in the *Giornale degli Economisti*,[65] put forward the idea that Sraffa's approach in terms of 'surplus' should not be mistaken for that of the classical economists, since Sraffa determined the prices of commodities without referring in any way to the labour-embodied value theory, and did not bring in any consideration of the market. Indeed, in Ricardo, the problem of the invariable standard could not be dissociated from the question of value, while in Sraffa this link had been entirely lost. This review opened the way, in Italy, to a long debate between Marxists and 'Sraffians' about the status of the theory of value in Marx and about the problem of the 'transformation' of values into production prices.

If, for certain Marxist economists, the work of Sraffa is absolutely incompatible with that of Marx, some authors, such as Meek or Dobb, have suggested possible convergences. Ronald M. Meek, in the *Scottish Journal of Political Economy*, asserts that:

> Sraffa is postulating precisely the same relation between the average rate of profits and the conditions of production in his 'standard' industry as Marx was postulating between the average rate of profits and the conditions of production in his industry of 'average organic composition of capital'.[66]

As for Dobb, his review, 'An Epoch-making Book', was published in the *Labour Monthly*,[67] the journal his friend Sraffa had contacted during his first stay in London. He asserted that *Production of Commodities by Means of Commodities* definitely solved the problem, which existed in Marx's work, of the 'transformation' of values into production prices, even if the author had not explicitly tackled this question in the appendix where he mentioned his 'sources'.

As Sraffa never published any work on Marx's economic theory, and had never given any explanation of this theory that might have clarified the aim of *Production of Commodities by Means of Commodities*, some of the economists who participated in the international debate on 'transformation' which took place in the sixties, and who had the opportunity to meet Sraffa, asked him whether he could clarify his point of view. The following, for example, is the account given by Gilles Dostaler of a conversation he had with Sraffa in Cambridge in June 1973. According to the Canadian economist, Sraffa asserted that his 'values' and Marx's 'production prices' in Volume 3 of *Capital* referred 'exactly to the same reality'. He added:

> Sraffa told us that he would not have been able to write *Production of Commodities by Means of Commodities* if Marx had not written *Capital*. It was clear, he told us, that he had been strongly influenced by the work of Marx, and that he felt more in sympathy with him than with those he called the 'whitewashers' of capitalist reality. Obviously aware of the criticism directed against him in certain Marxist circles, Sraffa explained to us that it was not his job to rewrite the three volumes of *Capital*. Moreover, Sraffa believed that his model described some aspects of the same reality that had been described by Marx's, a reality characterized by class antagonism between workers and capitalists, and the exploitation of workers by capitalists.[68]

LAST YEARS

In 1963 Sraffa, then sixty-five years old, retired from his post as Assistant Director of Research, but was an Emeritus Reader in Economics at Trinity College until 1965, and stayed on as Librarian at the Marshall Library of Economics until 1973. It was as a librarian that Sraffa's 'willing and active co-operation' was praised by John K. Whitaker, who, in 1971–74, was preparing an edition of Marshall's early writings in economics.[69] By the early sixties, Sraffa was beginning to feel that he could no longer devote himself to continuous research. In spring 1967 he told Luca Meldolesi that he had put together the scattered writings of Saint-Simon, whose work had, according to him, largely anticipated Marx's political theory, but that he did not have the strength to carry through a complete edition of his works.[70] He was at the time working on the *General Index* of his edition of Ricardo's *Collected Works*, Volume XI of the series, with the help of Arnold Heertje.[71]

During the sixties, many researchers were eager to meet Sraffa and to seek his advice. They were always warmly received in the bachelor's rooms, in Nevile's Court, which he had been given for life by Trinity College.[72] The young economists who came from Italy to see him included Salvatore Biasco,

Sebastiano Brusco, Giorgio Gilibert, Alfredo Medio, Luca Meldolesi, Guido Montani, Domenico–Mario Nuti, Alessandro Roncaglia and Fernando Vianello. Researchers from other countries included Amit Bhaduri, Krishna R. Bharadwaj, Arun Bose and Bertram Schefold. Sraffa was often asked to participate in international symposiums dedicated to his work, but always refused such invitations, on the pretext that his theses could only be discussed between two persons in a face to face situation!

Sraffa was always extremely modest and discreet about his work as an economist. In spite of the numerous requests made by his Italian admirers and friends, he was generally reluctant to have all or any of his writings assembled in book form. Thus in 1972 he refused an offer of the publishers Laterza of Bari to bring together his major articles in one volume.[73] In March 1973 the publishing house of Il Mulino in Bologna, which was preparing a series of texts by great contemporary economists, asked his permission to publish a book of his writings from the period 1922–62. Unusually Sraffa gave his consent to this enterprise, but unfortunately the book came out only after his death. In the same year Aurelio Macchioro suggested a very interesting project to the Istituto Editoriale Internazionale publishing house in Milan, which was at the time reprinting classics of political economy:

> Why not produce a volume outside the series, devoted to his writings ... even the historical introductions, and some of the historical notes on Ricardo? With some historico-critical introductions, especially as regards the theoretical (and social) environment of Cambridge before the Second World War? As to the editing, of course ... Sraffa himself, for example, could do it, like Croce, who prepared his own volume for the Ricciardi edition.[74]

Much later, after Sraffa's death, Il Mulino were able to go ahead with their project for a series on great contemporary economists and, in 1986, published the volume for which Sraffa had given his consent thirteen years before.[75] Eventually the collected works, writings and correspondence, will be published under the direction of Professor Garegnani of the University of Rome; it will then be possible to read the as yet unpublished manuscripts, such as the Cambridge lectures.

Although he was permanently resident in Britain, Sraffa never applied for British citizenship. He had lost his chair at Cagliari during the Fascist years, but was reinstated after the Second World War. Nevertheless he always refused to accept the corresponding salary, and gave it to the library to buy books on economics.

Piero Sraffa had decided that, after his death, his personal estate and library should be left to Trinity College, which had ensured him a tranquil life. On this point, Nicholas Kaldor noted:

> Though Sraffa was the son of a prosperous lawyer, he was only able to bring a small part of his father's fortune out of Italy. He disliked gambling, and was also against speculating on the Stock Market, not so much on principle, as out of a conviction that one is bound to lose on unsuccessful bets a large part of the gains made on successful outcomes. Hence his basic principle was to wait for the one occasion when a large speculative gain appeared to be absolutely certain, and then put all the money one can get hold of on this one gamble. The one occasion which appeared to him to satisfy these criteria occurred during the War when the price of Japanese bonds fell to a very low level – something between 5–10 per cent of their nominal value, or not more than 1–2 per cent if one also takes the likely value of unpaid interest payments into account. He was convinced that, however the War might end, the Japanese would fulfil all their foreign financial obligations, whether they were made to do it or not. Hence he put all his money into Japanese bonds, after careful investigation of which most of them appeared undervalued, and he must have made a gain of 40 to 50 times the money he put into it, when, after the War, Japan resumed servicing the bonds and paid the accumulated interest during the years of hostility. It is not known how much money he made on this transaction, but the College valued his bequest at £1.5 million in 1983, one half consisting of the value of his library.[76]

In 1981, Piero Sraffa suffered a thrombosis and had to move permanently to the Hope clinic in Cambridge. After two years of suffering, he died on 3 September 1983, only a month after his old friend Joan Robinson.[77]

Postscript

At the end of this short book, which the reader will perhaps recognize as an attempt at a 'personal' biography, rather than a 'professional', or 'environmental' one,[1] I wish again to stress its incomplete and preliminary character. Much deeper research still has to be done, particularly in the Cambridge archives, in order to increase our knowledge of this very enigmatic figure. I only hope that this modest essay will encourage the reader to tackle Sraffa's writings himself and that it may then be used as a reading guide.

Notes

PREFACE

1. In fact this book began as a paper (uncompleted) dealing with their friendship. I started my research on this subject during the years 1977–78. I was then able to meet two old collaborators on the *L'Ordine Nuovo* who have since died, and to question them about the young Piero Sraffa: Andrea Viglongo in Turin, and Alfonso Leonetti in Rome.
2. Other archives were consulted, including, for example, the Joseph Schumpeter Archives, Harvard University Archives, Cambridge, Mass.

1. THE FORMATIVE YEARS

1. David Weatherall: *David Ricardo: A Biography*, The Hague, Martinus Nijhoff, 1976, p.2.
2. Some of our information about Angelo Sraffa comes from the obituary by Lorenzo Mossa, one of his students, who had rallied to Fascism and was a theorist of corporatism: 'Angelo Sraffa', *Rivista del Diritto Commerciale e del Diritto Generale delle Obbligazioni*, Vol. XXXVI, I, 1938, 1 part, pp. 7–18. One can also refer to the article 'Sraffa, Angelo' of *Enciclopedia italiana di scienze, lettere ed arte*, Rome: Instituto della Enciclopedia Italiana da Giovanni Treccani, Vol. XXXII, 1931, p. 430.
3. As a Mazzinian republican, Carducci rallied to the monarchy, convinced that it would be able to bring about Italian unity. As a professor at Bologna, he published many volumes of poetry, such as *Rime e ritmi* (1888–98) and *Odi barbare* (1861–87). In Pisa, he gave the famous speech 'Truth as Machiavellianism'.
4. After the death of his father, Piero Sraffa sold this library to Hoepli, the Milan bookseller-publisher (P. Sraffa: letter to L. Einaudi, 14 April 1938, preserved at the Einaudi Foundation in Turin).
5. The *Archivio Giuridico*, founded in 1862, published in 1872–74 the renowned study by Vito Cusumano (1843–1908), an adherent of the German historical school, 'Sulla condizione attuale degli studi economici in Germania', the first Italian study dealing with Marx's *Capital* on the basis of a 'direct reading'.
6. Florence: Pellas, 1891.
7. Pisa: Spoerri, 1894.

8. Florence: Cammelli, 1897.
9. Luigi L. Pasinetti: 'Piero Sraffa (1898–1983) breve saggio bio-bibliografico', *Economia Politica* (Bologna), 2nd year, no 3, December 1985, p. 333.
10. *Del mandato commerciale e della commissione: Commentario al Codice di commercio*, Milan: Vallardi, 1900, 2. edition 1934. One other essay might also be mentioned, *Studi di diritto commerciale*, Florence: Cammelli, 1907.
11. In 1903, its name was *Rivista di Diritto Commerciale, Industriale e Marittimo*; the name changed in 1910 to *Rivista del Diritto Commerciale e del Diritto Generale delle Obbligazioni*. This journal has appeared regularly since its inception, and still exists today.
12. This important institute published, from 1921 to 1938, an annual volume of forecasts about the Italian economy, the *Prospettive economiche*, prepared under the direction of Giorgio Mortara.
13. Mariano D'Amelio, born in Naples, dedicated himself, before the First World War, to the setting up of legal reforms for the Italian colony of Eritrea. In 1919–20, he was to delegate to the Peace Conference in Paris. In 1923, he became, thanks to the Fascist regime, First President of the Italian Court of Appeal, after unification with the regional courts, then, in 1924, Senator and Vice-president of the Senate.
14. Libero Lenti: 'Gli ottant'anni della Bocconi', *Nuova Antologia* (Florence), 118th year, vol. 552, No. 2148, October–December 1983, p. 244.
15. In 1938, Angelo's son gave the Bocconi University his valuable law library, and, in December 1961, his collection of literary works, from which the works of Carducci had already been removed (cf supra, note 4). See Sraffa's letter to Einaudi, undated, but most probably sent at the end of 1961, and preserved at the Einaudi Foundation in Turin.
16. It is difficult at present to determine whether Piero Sraffa could have had knowledge of other anti-positivist or anti-rationalist movements imported into Italy during that period, e. g. the ideas of William James and Henri Bergson.
17. See B. Croce: *Ciò che è vivo e ciò che è morto nella filosofia di Hegel* (1906).
18. A. Gramsci: 'Problemi di oggi e di domani', *L'Ordine Nuovo*, 3 series, no 3–4, 1–15 April 1924, reprinted in Gramsci, *La costruzione del Partito Comunista: 1923–6*, Turin: Einaudi, 1971, p. 179.
19. A. Roncaglia: *Sraffa e la teoria dei prezzi*, Bari: Laterza, 2. edition 1981, Appendix 'La rivoluzione di Sraffa', p. 171.
20. 'Il socialismo degli imbroglioni'. Interesting indications about the political stance of Cosmo can be found in Gramsci's paper, 'Franche parole ad un borghese', *Avanti!* , 5 November 1920, reproduced in *L'Ordine Nuovo: 1919–1920*, Turin: Einaudi, 1987, pp. 758–61.
21. Cosmo taught Angelo Tasca, founder in 1909 of Fascio Giovanile Socialista, Centro di Torino, and Umberto Terracini at the Gioberti school in Turin, as extraordinary professor. Gramsci was one of his students at the Faculty of Literature at Turin, where he gave some lectures.
22. P. Sraffa: letter to A. Gramsci, February or March 1924, partly published by Gramsci in 'Problemi di oggi e di domani', *L'Ordine Nuovo*, 3 series, no 3–4, 1–15 April 1924, reprinted in Gramsci, *La costruzione del Partito Comunista: 1923–6*, Turin: Einaudi, 1971, p. 175.
23. About the work of Achille Loria, see Jean-Pierre Potier: *Lectures italiennes de Marx: Les conflits d'interprétation chez les économistes et les philosophes, 1883–1983*, Lyon: Presses Universitaires de Lyon, 1986, pp. 68–101.

24. See, for this aspect, Riccardo Faucci, 'Fra Einaudi e Gramsci: Sraffa e la cultura economica italiana degli anni venti', in *Tra teoria economica e grande cultura europea: Piero Sraffa*, Riccardo Bellofiore, ed., Milan: F. Angeli, 1986, p. 20.
25. John Eatwell and Carlo Panico: 'Sraffa, Piero (1898–1983)', in *The New Palgrave: A Dictionary of Economics*, J. Eatwell, M. Milgate, P. Newman, eds., London: Macmillan, Vol. IV, 1987, p. 445.
26. A. Gramsci: letter to his sister-in-law, Tatiana Schucht, 23 February 1931, in *Gramsci's Prison Letters: Lettere dal Carcere*, London: Zwan, 1988, p. 138; see also the conversation with Sraffa reported by Maria-Antonietta Macciocchi in *Pour Gramsci*, Paris: Le Seuil, 1974, p. 288.
27. Palmiro Togliatti had defended in Turin, in 1915, under the supervision of Einaudi, a doctoral thesis in political economy, 'Il regime doganale delle colonie'.
28. In April 1920 the employers took advantage of the change to summer time to compel the workers to start an hour earlier; this was the pretext for the strike.
29. About the period, see P. Spriano's book, *L'occupazione delle fabbriche*, Turin: Einaudi, 1968; see also Giuseppe Maione, *Il biennio rosso: Autonomia e spontaneità operaia nel 1919–20*, Bologna: Il Mulino, 1975.
30. I was unable to trace these translations in the first series of *L'Ordine Nuovo*.
31. A former member of that circle, Attilio Segre, remembered Sraffa's participation. His testimony appeared in the collection edited by Mimma Paulesu Quercioli, *Gramsci vivo nelle testimonianze dei suoi contemporanei*, Milan: Feltrinelli, 1977, p. 142. Moreover, one of the best childhood friends of Gramsci, Andrea Viglongo, personally confirmed to me, in September 1977, Sraffa's adherence to that group.
32. The Luigi Einaudi Foundation has the original typescript of the thesis (sixty-four pages), with a few hand-written corrections by the author; on the flyleaf can be found the annotations which Einaudi had prepared for the *viva*. The quotations come from this original (classification R.16.5.23). The thesis was printed in 1920 by the Premiata Scuola Tipografica Salesiana in Milan.
33. *L'inflazione monetaria in Italia durante e dopo la guerra*, p. 34.
34. *Ibid*., p. 48 and ff.
35. *Ibid*., p. 64.
36. Fubini published, later on, a new Italian translation of some of the works of Ricardo (Turin: UTET).
37. A. Roncaglia: 'Piero Sraffa: una bibliografia ragionata', *Studi Economici*, 38th year, no 21, 1983, p. 138; 'Sraffa e le banche', *Rivista Milanese di Economia*, no 10, April–June 1984, p. 108.
38. T. E. Gregory published a two volume compilation in 1929, *Select Statutes, Documents and Reports relating to British Banking: 1832–1928*, London: Oxford University Press.
39. Edwin Cannan published, in 1893, the important work, *A History of the Theories of Production and Distribution in English Political Economy from 1776 to 1848*, and in 1929, *A Review of Economic Theory*, London: King.
40. See Chapter 2, pp. 21–2.
41. This villa, owned today by Harvard University, houses an International Study Centre of art history.
42. In 1906, Mary Berenson asked her sister, Alys Smith, first wife of Bertrand Russell, to find two young men who could accompany her two daughters, Ray and Karin Costelloe, born of a previous marriage, to the family villa, during the

Easter holidays. One of the young men was John Maynard Keynes, then aged twenty-three, and a student at Oxford; he fell 'a little bit' in love with the eldest daughter, Ray (seventeen years old), but afterwards 'his interest in Ray was eclipsed by a more intense feeling for the forty-two year old mother', Meryle Secrest: *Being Bernard Berenson: A Critical Biography*, New York: Holt, Rinehart and Winston, 1979, p.324 Reference can also be made to the two following books: Robert Skidelsky: *John Maynard Keynes: A Biography*, Vol. 1, *Hopes Betrayed: 1883–1920*, London: Macmillan, 1983, Charles H. Hession: *John Maynard Keynes*, New York: Macmillan, 1983, pp. 79–80. After that episode, Keynes kept up close contact with the Berenson family and visited them at I Tatti, especially in 1910, 1911 and 1920.

43. This letter is among the Keynes Papers in the Marshall Library, at Cambridge University. It was published in English in *Keynes in Italia: Catalogo bibliografico*, edited by the Facoltà di Economia e Commercio, Università di Firenze, in the Banca Toscana series, Studi e Informazioni, no 7, 1983, p. 163.
44. See P. Sraffa: letter to L. Einaudi, 30 November 1921, and the postcard dated 4 February 1922, which mentions an exchange of reviews, *Economica v. La Riforma Sociale*. These documents are preserved at the Luigi Einaudi Foundation in Turin.
45. This bank, founded in 1915, primarily financed the military activities of the Ansaldo group.
46. P. Sraffa: 'The Bank Crisis in Italy', *Economic Journal*, Vol. XXXII, June 1922, p. 197.
47. A. Roncaglia: *Sraffa e la teoria dei prezzi*, Bari: Laterza, 2. edition, 1981. Appendix, 'La rivoluzione di Sraffa', p. 174.
48. *The Manchester Guardian Commercial, Reconstruction in Europe*, Supplement no XI, 7 December 1922, pp. 675–6.
49. Sraffa reported this telegram from Mussolini in a letter to Keynes dated Christmas 1922 which has been preserved among the Keynes Papers in the Marshall Library, quoted by Nicholas Kaldor, 'Piero Sraffa (1898–1983)', *Proceedings of the British Academy*, Vol. LXXI, 1985, p. 618.
50. C. Panico, 'Sraffa on money and banking', *Cambridge Journal of Economics*, Vol. 12, no 1, March 1988, p. 17, note 2 .
51. Luca Meldolesi: *L'utopia realmente esistente: Marx e Saint-Simon*, Bari: Latera, 1982, Appendix, 'Piero Sraffa e il marxismo', p. 110.
52. Officially, Italy and England were still on good terms at that time. Consequently, the English had to respect the Italian list of undesirable people.
53. J. M. Keynes: letter to Davidson, 29 January 1923, quoted by Pier-Luigi Porta in 'Piero Sraffa (1898–1983)', *Rivista Internazionale di Scienze Economiche e Commerciali* (Milan), 31st year, no 1, January 1984, p. 16.
54. J. M. Keynes: letter to Davidson, 29 February 1923, quoted by Nicholas Kaldor in 'Piero Sraffa (1898–1983)', *Proceedings of the British Academy*, Vol. LXXI, 1985, p. 619.
55. About this, see pp. 15–16.
56. Italics in the original, 'Opinioni', *La Rivoluzione Liberale*, 2nd year, no 31, 16 October 1923, p. 128, simply signed 'S' and attributed by me to Sraffa. This article does not figure among the list of works, published by Alessandro Roncaglia in *Sraffa e la teoria dei prezzi*, Laterza, 2. edition, 1981, pp. 185–8, neither does it figure in the list that can be found at the end of Sraffa's collection, *Saggi*, Bologna: Il Mulino, 1986, pp. 265–70.

57. Fabio Ranchetti: 'Mattioli "economista critico"', *Rivista di Storia Economica* (Venice), new series, Vol. III, no 2, June 1986, p. 231.
58. Mattioli translated into Italian, possibly prompted by Sraffa, Keynes's article 'The Stabilization of the European Exchanges: a Plan for Genoa', *The Manchester Guardian Commercial, Reconstruction in Europe*, supplement no I, 20 April 1922, republished in Keynes, *Activities 1920–1922: Treaty Revision and Reconstruction, The Collected Writings*, Vol. XVII, Macmillan and Cambridge University Press, 1977, pp. 355–69; Italian translation, 'La "stabilizzazione" dei cambri europei', *Rivista Bancaria*, May 1922.
59. Carlo Rosselli: letter to his mother, 21 July 1923, in *Epistolario familiare: Carlo, Nello Rosselli e la madre (1914–1937)*, Zeffiro Ciuffoletti, ed., Milan: Sugarco, 1979, p. 172. In 1924, he was appointed to a professorship at the Higher Institute of Genoa.
60. C. Rosselli: letter to his mother, 17 January 1924, in *ibid.*, p. 207.
61. Anna Kuliscioff: letter to Filippo Turati, 9 June 1924, and Turati: letter to Kuliscioff, 10 June 1924, in Turati and Kuliscioff, *Carteggio*, Vol. VI, *1923–1925, Il delitto Matteotti e l'Aventino*, Turin: Einaudi, 1977, resp. pp. 280 and 284.
62. Some references to this institute can be found in the letters of Kuliscioff to Turati (18 June 1925) and of Turati to Kuliscioff (22 August 1925) in *ibid.*, respt. pp. 718 and 749. After the assassination of Matteotti, Rosselli joined the USP in July of the same year; the party was disbanded by the Fascists in November 1925.
63. See, for example, Nicolà Tranfaglia: *Carlo Rosselli dall' interventismo a 'Giustizia e Libertà*, Bari: Laterza, 1968, p. 168, note 25, and Z. Ciuffoletti, in *Epistolario familiare: Carlo, Nello Rosselli e la madre (1914–1937)*, Milan: Sugarco, 1979, note p. 190.
64. The existence of this journey is known through the Sraffa-Einaudi correspondence preserved at the Luigi Einaudi Foundation in Turin.
65. 'Obituary: Maffeo Pantaleoni', *Economic Journal*, Vol. XXXIV, December 1924, pp. 648–53. The paper by Loria follows, pp. 653–4.
66. *Ibid.*, pp. 650–1.
67. Alfred Marshall: 'The Pure Theory of Foreign Trade', and 'The Pure Theory of Domestic Values' (private publication, 1879).
68. *La riforma monetaria*, Milan: Treves, 1925.
69. He may have been contacted by Giorgio Mortara, professor at the Bocconi University. The information which follows comes from the bibliography of Sraffa's works by Pierangelo Garegnani and at the end of the collection *Saggi*, Bologna: Il Mulino, 1986, p. 268.
70. Boston: Houghton Mifflin, 1923. *Giornale degli Economisti e Rivista di Statistica* (Rome), 4 series, 40th year, Vol. LXV, 1925, pp. 389–90.
71. R. A. Lehfeldt, *Money*, London: Oxford University Press, 1926; M. Segre, *Le banche nell' ultimo decennio, con particolare riguardo al loro sviluppo patologico nel dopo guerra*, Milan: La Stampa Commerciale, 1926. *Giornale degli Economisti e Rivista di Statistica*, 4th series, 41st year, Vol. LXVI, 1926, p. 230.
72. London: Macdonald and Evans, 1926. *Giornale degli Economisti e Rivista di Statistica*, 4 series, 42nd year, Vol. LXVII, 1927, p. 610.
73. Alfred Marshall died in 1924, and Keynes devoted a study to him: 'Alfred Marshall – 1842–1924' in the *Economic Journal*, September 1924, reprinted in

Keynes, *Essays in Biography* (1933), *The Collected Writings*, Vol. X, Macmillan and Cambridge University Press, 1972, pp. 161–231.

74. *Annali di Economia* (Milan), Vol. II, 1925, pp. 277–328.
75. Graziadei was expelled from the university in 1926, and was for a time under house arrest; he then took up once more his critical studies of Marx, which he managed to get published under the fascist regime; this caused him, in 1928, to be expelled from the Italian Communist Party for 'treason', but he was reinstated in 1945. Concerning the theses of Graziadei, see Jean-Pierre Potier, *Lectures italiennes de Marx: Les conflits d'interprétation chez les économistes et les philosophes, 1883–1983*, Lyon: Presses Universitaires de Lyon, 1986, pp. 113–27.
76. Rome: Maglione e Strini, 1925. Giorgio Gattei: 'In merito ad un possibile rapporto tra Sraffa e Graziadei', in Roberto Finzi, ed., *Neo-Ricardiana: Sraffa e Graziadei*, Bologna: Il Mulino, 1977, pp. 216–17. The letter is kept at the Biblioteca Comunale of Imola (Antonio Graziadei's letters).
77. Lorenzo Mossa published *L'impresa nell' ordine corporativo*, Florence: Sansoni, 1935.
78. Of a liberal bent, Giuseppe-Ugo Papi, soon to publish the famous *Lezioni di economia politica* (1932) and future Rector, was at that time teaching at the university and at the Higher Institute of Commercial Studies in Rome.
79. Carlo Grilli, doctor of Perugia University, had followed, in Paris, the courses of Charles Gide. He was the author of a study on *The Protectionist Colonial Experiments in neo-Latin Africa after the War*.
80. Angelo Fraccacreta published, among other things, a study of the labour movement in French agriculture.
81. 'Relazione della commissione giudicatrice del concorso per professore non stabile alla cattedra di economia politica nella R. Università di Cagliari', in Ministero della Pubblica Istruzione: *Bollettino Ufficiale*, Parte II, *Atti di amministrazione* (Rome), 53rd year, Vol. I, no 9, 4 March 1926, p. 776. All the information about the competition comes from this document.
82. Letter preserved in the Keynes Papers, Marshall Library, Cambridge, of which three important extracts have been published by Roncaglia, *Sraffa and the Theory of Prices*, Chichester, etc.: John Wiley and Sons, 1978, pp. 11–13.
83. 'The Laws of Returns under Competitive Conditions', *Economic Journal*, Vol. XXXVI, December 1926, pp. 535–50.
84. *Ibid.*, p. 543.
85. See below, p. 45.
86. *Op. cit.*, p. 535.
87. This journal was published in Florence from January to October 1925.
88. J. M. Keynes: letter to P. Sraffa, 25 January 1927, preserved in the Keynes Papers, Marshall Library, quoted by Nicholas Kaldor, 'Piero Sraffa (1898–1983)', *Proceedings of the British Academy*, Vol. LXXI, 1985, p. 624–25.
89. *Ibid.*, p. 626.

2. AFFINITIES WITH COMMUNISM

1. The Partito Comunista d'Italia was founded at the Congress of Livorno in January 1921 and was led, until 1923, by the engineer Amadeo Bordiga (1896–1970).

2. 'How the American bourgeoisie fights labour organization – Boycott and spying – How a strike is broken – The "yellow dog"'.
3. 'Open Shop Drive', *L'Ordine Nuovo*, 2 series, 5 July 1921, p. 3. In his *Prison Notebooks* Gramsci, while commenting on 'Fordism', alluded to the problem raised by this article; he mentioned that the 'Rotary Club organized the campaign for the Open Shop and, in consequence, for rationalization' (*Quaderni del Carcere*, Turin: Einaudi, 1975, Notebook 5, Vol. 1, p. 541; see also Vol. 4, note 1, pp. 2667–8).
4. 'Industriali e governo inglese contro i lavoratori', *L'Ordine Nuovo*, 2 series, 24 July 1921, p. 3.
5. P. Sraffa, 'I "Labour Leaders"', *L'Ordine Nuovo*, 2 series, 4 August 1921, p. 1.
6. I got this information from Viglongo himself, whom I met in Turin in September 1977. His recollections about that episode can be found in the compilation edited by Mimma Paulesu Quercioli, *Gramsci vivo nelle testimonianze dei suoi contemporanei*, Feltrinelli, 1977, p. 172. As regards Viglongo's activities, see Giancarlo Bergami's book, *Il giovane Gramsci e il marxismo*, 1911–18, Milan: Feltrinelli, 1977, esp. pp. 143–8.
7. During his stay in the USSR, which ended in December 1923, Gramsci met his future wife, Giulia Schucht.
8. P. Sraffa, letter partially published in 'Problemi di oggi e di domani', *L'Ordine Nuovo*, 3 series, 1st year, no 3–4, 1–15 April 1924, reprinted in A. Gramsci, *La costruzione del Partito Comunista: 1923–6*, Turin: Einaudi, 1971, pp. 175–6.
9. *Ibid.*, pp. 177 and 179–80.
10. According to Gramsci, Sraffa's ideas would be very close to those of the Italian Socialist Party, which were those of the 'maximalists' after the expulsion of the 'reformists' at the congress in Rome, in October 1922.
11. The subtitle of the 3 series of *L'Ordine Nuovo* is *Rassegna di politica e di cultura operaia*.
12. A. Gramsci: letter to Togliatti, Scoccimaro, Leonetti, etc., 21 March 1924, in Togliatti, *La formazione del gruppo dirigente del P. C. I. nel 1923–1924*, Rome: Riuniti, 1962, pp. 241–3. In 1927, the Italian Communist Party defended the idea of an underground trade union, and tried to reconstitute a Confederazione Generale del Lavoro. But when confronted with the difficulties of the task, it preferred, from 1929 on, to infiltrate the Fascist trade unions.
13. Gramsci owned a collection of these volumes.
14. A. Gramsci: 'Un esame della situazione italiana', reprinted in its entirety in Gramsci, *La costruzione del Partito Comunista: 1923–26*, Turin: Einaudi, 1971, pp. 113–24.
15. P. Sraffa: letter to Gramsci's sister-in-law, Tatiana Schucht, 23 August 1931, in *Nuove lettere di Antonio Gramsci con altre lettere di Piero Sraffa*, Rome: Riuniti, 1986, pp. 59–60. This information was passed on to Gramsci by Tatiana Schucht on 28 August 1931. (See A. Gramsci, *Lettere dal Carcere*, Turin: Einaudi, 1965, p. 483, note 1.)
16. A. Gramsci: letter to P. Sraffa, 11 December 1926, in A. Gramsci, *Lettere dal Carcere*, Einaudi, 1965, p. 15.
17. This he told to Gramsci in a letter dated 13 December 1926, most probably lost today, mentioned in a letter dated 17 December 1926 which he received from the prisoner ('I am very thankful for your kindness') and in a letter from Gramsci to Tatiana Schucht dated 19 December 1926, in *Lettere dal Carcere*, Einaudi, 1965, resp. pp. 16 and 23. Sraffa kept two lists of the books which were sent at

that time, published in Appendix I of *Lettere dal Carcere*, Einaudi, 1965, pp. 609–12.

18. Alfred Marshall, *Principia di economia*, Turin: UTET, 1905 (4 series of the 'Biblioteca dell' Economista') republished in 1925.
19. Richard Lewinsohn, *Histoire de l'inflation: Le déplacement de la richesse en Europe (1914–1925)*, translated from the German, Paris: Payot, 1926.
20. Turin: Edizioni di *La Riforma Sociale*, 1926.
21. This document is attached to a letter from Bordiga to Gramsci, dated 27 January 1927, published in the Appendix of the article by Valentino Gerratana, 'Note di filologia gramsciana', *Studi Storici* (Rome), 16th year, no 1, January–March 1975, p. 146, note 2.
22. Graziadei had also sent a copy of this book to Sraffa, who thanked the author in a letter of 18 June 'for the volume, which interests me greatly, and which I am taking to Cagliari to read during the exams' (letter published in an article by Giorgio Gattei, 'In merito ad un possibile rapporto tra Sraffa e Graziadei', in Roberto Finzi, ed., *Neo-Ricardiana: Sraffa e Graziadei*, Bologna: Il Mulino, 1977, p. 217).
23. Paolo Spriano: 'Gli ultimi anni di Gramsci in un colloquio con Piero Sraffa', *Rinascita* (Rome), no 15, 14 April 1967, p. 14; Gramsci: letter to Tatiana Schucht, 14 July 1929, in *Gramsci's Prison Letters: Lettere dal Carcere*, London: Zwan, 1988, p.103.
24. Camilla Ravera: *Diario di trent' anni: 1913–1943*, Rome: Riuniti, 1973, p. 267.
25. This was the start of a regular correspondence between the two friends. In the following chapter, we will examine the discussion about the 'quota novanta' and the publication of Labriola's letters to Engels.
26. P. Sraffa: letter to A. Tasca, from London, 22 September 1927, preserved at the Feltrinelli Foundation in Milan, published in *Rinascita* (Rome), no 31, 4 August 1978, pp. 24–5.
27. A. Tasca: letter to P. Sraffa, 2 October 1927, preserved at the Feltrinelli Foundation in Milan.
28. A. Tasca: letter to P. Sraffa, 5 October 1927, preserved at the Feltrinelli Foundation in Milan.
29. P. Sraffa: letter to A. Tasca, 15 October 1927, preserved at the Feltrinelli Foundation in Milan. He may have been helped in his task by his new friend Maurice Dobb.
30. 'Correspondence, The Methods of Fascism: The Case of Antonio Gramsci', *The Manchester Guardian*, 24 October 1927, reproduced in Gramsci, *Lettere dal Carcere*, Turin: Einaudi, 1965, Appendix 2, p. 913. 'Mr Shaw' is of course the writer George Bernard Shaw. The entire document has been wrongly attributed to Sraffa.
31. P. Sraffa: letter to A. Tasca, 30 April 1928, preserved at the Feltrinelli Foundation in Milan.
32. A. Gramsci: letter to Tatiana Schucht, 14 July 1929, in *Gramsci's Prison Letters: Lettere dal Carcere*, London: Zwan, 1988, p. 103.
33. This contact is clearly brought out in the letter from Sraffa to Togliatti dated 26 December 1928, published in *Rinascita* (Rome), no 13, 1 April 1977, p. 20.
34. Camilla Ravera: *Diario di trent' anni: 1913–1943*, Rome: Riuniti, 1973, pp. 434 and 495.
35. About the political itinerary of Angelo Tasca, see Alexander J. De Grand: *Angelo Tasca: Un politico scomodo*, Milan: Franco Angeli, 1985.

36. Not long after, Leonetti and Ravazzoli made contact with Leon Trotsky. During the interview that he gave me in Rome in June 1978, Leonetti declared that he had sent Sraffa the *Bollettino dell' Opposizione*, which had been coming out since 1931, but without ever getting an answer from him.
37. References to these episodes can be found in Ferdinando Ormea, *Le origini dello stalinismo nel P. C. I. : Storia della 'svolta' comunista degli anni trenta*, Milan: Feltrinelli, 1978.
38. Brian H. Pollitt: 'The Collaboration of Maurice Dobb in Sraffa's Edition of Ricardo', *Cambridge Journal of Economics*, Vol. 12, no 1, March 1988, p. 58. They returned together to the USSR at Easter 1952 for an international economics conference; *op. cit.*, p. 63, note 2.
39. Giorgio Amendola: 'Gramsci-Togliatti, negli anni della Svolta', *Rinascita Sarda*, March 1967, republished in Amendola, *Comunismo, anti-fascismo, resistenza*, Rome: Riuniti, 1967 ('Le lettere di Gramsci'), pp. 433–7; Giorgia Amendola, *Un' isola*, Milan: Rizzoli, 1980, French translation: *L' ile: Mémoires d' un exil*, Paris: Liana Lévi et Sylvie Messinger, 1983, pp. 41–3.
40. *L' île: Mémoires d' un exil, op. cit.*, pp. 74–5.
41. This episode is related by Sraffa in Paolo Spriano, 'Gli ultimi anni di Gramsci in un colloquio con Piero Sraffa', *Rinascita*, no 15, 14 April 1967, p. 14.
42. On Gramsci's Marxism, see Jean-Pierre Potier: *Lectures italiennes de Marx: Les conflits d' interprétation chez les économistes et les philosophes, 1883–1983*, Lyon: Presses Universitaires de Lyon, 1986, pp. 201–65.
43. At the end of 1931, the prisoner was no longer allowed to receive foreign publications.
44. Umberto Cosmo: *Vita di Dante*, Bari: Laterza, 1930.
45. A. Gramsci: letter to Tatiana Schucht, 23 February 1931, in *Gramsci's Prison Letters: Lettere dal Carcere*, London: Zwan, 1988, pp. 137–8.
46. A. Gramsci: letter to Tatiana Schucht, 17 August 1931, in *Gramsci's Prison Letters: Lettere dal Carcere*, London: Zwan, 1988, p. 156. The passage about Cosmo was sent to Gramsci by Sraffa. The text of Cosmo's letter of 10 August was published in *Lettere dal Carcere*, Einaudi, 1965, pp. 616–17, note 2.
47. A. Gramsci: letters to Tatiana Schucht, 7 and 20 September 1931, in *Gramsci's Prison Letters: Lettere dal Carcere*, London: Zwan, 1988, resp. pp. 162 and 168. The reflections on Canto X of Dante's *Inferno* can be found in Notebook 4, *Quaderni del Carcere*, Einaudi, 1975, pp. 516–30.
48. U. Cosmo: letter to P. Sraffa, 29 December 1931, in *Lettere dal Carcere*, Einaudi, 1965, pp. 593–4, note 1. Gramsci was 'quite satisfied with the knowledge that the interpretation of the canto which I have sketched out is relatively new and worthy of more detailed treatment', letter to Tatiana Schucht, 21 March 1932, in *Gramsci's Prison Letters: Lettere dal Carcere*, London: Zwan, 1988, p. 201.
49. A. Gramsci: letter to Tatiana Schucht, 14 March 1932, in *op. cit.*, p. 199. See also *Quaderni del Carcere*, Einaudi, 1975, Notebook 8, p. 985, Notebook 13, p. 1575.
50. P. Sraffa: letter to Tatiana Schucht, 21 April 1932, preserved at the Feltrinelli Foundation in Milan.
51. The answer by Sraffa was sent in its entirety by Tatiana Schucht in her letter to Gramsci dated 27 April 1932, in *Lettere dal Carcere*, Einaudi, 1965, pp. 616–17, note 2.
52. See A. Gramsci: letter to Tatiana Schucht, 2 May 1932, in *Gramsci's Prison Letters: Lettere dal Carcere*, London: Zwan, 1988, p. 213. Gramsci transcribed

Sraffa's answer in his *Prison Notebooks* (*Quaderni del Carcere*, Einaudi, 1975, Notebook 8, p. 1038).

53. Bari: Laterza, 1931. See below, p. 57.
54. Quoted letter of 21 June 1932, preserved at the Gramsci Foundation in Rome.
55. See for example Franco De Felice, 'Nord e Sud nel pensiero di Rodolfo Morandi: Dalla *Storia della grande industria* alla Resistenza', *Rivista Storica del Socialismo*, 7th year, no 21, January–April 1964, pp. 21–67. De Felice saw in this book a 'history of northern industry' that neglected to examine the South; the southern question was not viewed 'as a specific form, as a component of Italian capitalism' (*op. cit.*, esp. pp. 27–9).
56. 'Intorno alla storia recente della grande industria italiana', signed XXX, in *La Riforma Sociale*, Vol. XXXIX, no 3, May–June 1932, pp. 318–21. See Gramsci, *Quaderni del Carcere*, Einaudi, 1975, Notebook 9, pp. 1176–7. These notes can also be found in Notebook 19, Einaudi, 1975, pp. 1991–5.
57. See below, pp. 63 and ff.
58. A. Gramsci: letter to Tatiana Schucht, 28 September 1931, in *Gramsci's Prison Letters: Lettere dal Carcere*, London: Zwan, 1988, p. 169.
59. This reply of Sraffa's was passed on in a letter from Tatiana Schucht to Gramsci dated 2 February 1932, in *Lettere dal Carcere*, Turin: Einaudi, 1975, p. 570–1, note 1.
60. A. Gramsci: letter to Tatiana Schucht, 8 February 1932, in *Gramsci's Prison Letters: Lettere dal Carcere*, London: Zwan, 1988, p. 190–1.
61. Tatiana Schucht: letter to A. Gramsci, 18 March 1932, in *Lettere dal Carcere*, Einaudi, 1965, pp. 594–5, note 2.
62. A. Gramsci: letter to Tatiana Schucht, 21 March 1932, in *op cit.*, p. 201. The following year, Gramsci again took up his idea about the absence of antisemitism in Italy, in a commentary to a review of Cecil Roth's book *Gli Ebrei in Venezia*, which had been translated not long before (see *Quaderni del Carcere*, Einaudi, 1975, Notebook 15, pp. 1800–1).
63. *Science at the Crossroads* (papers presented to the International Congress of the History of Science and Technology held in London from 29 June to 3 July 1931 by the delegates of the USSR), London: Kniga, 1931. (cf. the article by Dino Ferreri, 'Como si è formata l'edizione critica', *Rinascita*, no 30, 25 July 1975, p. 14.) This book contains a contribution by Nicolai Bukharin, 'Theory and practice from the standpoint of dialectic materialism', to which Gramsci made reference in his *Notebooks*.
64. P. Sraffa: letter to Tatiana Schucht, 23 August 1931, in *Nuove lettere di Antonio Gramsci con altre lettere di Piero Sraffa*, Rome: Riuniti, 1986, p. 61. These remarks were passed on to Gramsci by Tatiana Schucht on 28 August 1931.
65. Bari: Laterza, 1932.
66. A. Gramsci: letter to Tatiana Schucht, 18 April 1932, in *Gramsci's Prison Letters: Lettere dal Carcere*, London: Zwan, 1988, p. 210.
67. P. Sraffa: letter to Tatiana Schucht, 16 May 1932, preserved at the Gramsci Foundation in Rome.
68. 'Club' is used by Gramsci in the sense of the club of Hercules.
69. A. Gramsci: letter to Tatiana Schucht, 2 May 1932, *Gramsci's Prison Letters: Lettere dal Carcere*, London: Zwan, 1988, pp. 213–14.
70. A. Gramsci: letter to Tatiana Schucht, 9 May 1932, in *op. cit.*, pp. 215–16.
71. A. Gramsci: letter to Tatiana Schucht, 6 June 1932, in *op. cit.*, pp. 221–2 .

72. P. Sraffa: letter to Tatiana Schucht, 21 June 1932, preserved at the Gramsci Foundation in Rome.
73. A. Gramsci: 'Alcuni temi della questione meridionale', originally published in *Lo Stato Operaio* (Paris), 4th year, no 1, January 1930, reprinted in Gramsci: *La questione meridionale*, Rome: Riuniti, 1970.
74. Eduard Bernstein, 'Presuppositions of Socialism and the Tasks of Social Democracy' (1899), published as *Evolutionary Socialism: a Criticism and Affirmation*, New York: Schocken Books, 1975.
75. See *La Critica* (Naples), Vol. XXV, no 5, 20 September 1927, p. 311, taken up again in Georges Sorel, *Lettere a Benedetto Croce*, Bari: De Donato, 1980, p. 86.
76. P. Sraffa: letter to Tatiana Schucht, 21 June 1932, preserved at the Gramsci Foundation in Rome.
77. Paris: Ed. Jacques, 1906.
78. The text of Arcangeli's certificate is published in Gramsci, *Lettere dal Carcere*, Einaudi, 1965, p. 763.
79. See Togliatti's letter to Sraffa dated 24 May 1933, published in *Rinascita*, no 13, 1 April 1977, p. 20; see also Angelo Sraffa's letter of 29 May 1933 to his son, published in the same review; these letters have been reproduced by Paolo Spriano in *Gramsci in carcere e il partito*, Rome: Riuniti, 1977, pp. 149–52.
80. *Op. cit.*, pp. 65 and 69–70.
81. *Ibid.*, pp. 69-and 73–6.
82. Permission to visit depended in fact on Benito Mussolini.
83. Gramsci tried to do more work on his *Notebooks*; he put together earlier scattered notes, but for the most part did little more than copy them without many changes.
84. P. Spriano: *Gramsci in carcere e il partito*, Riuniti, 1977, pp. 82–3.
85. Alfonso Leonetti: 'Gramsci, Togliatti e le confessioni', *Il Ponte*, 31 July–31 August 1975, p. 783, quoted by Ferdinando Ormea in *Le origini dello stalinismo nel P. C. I.*, Feltrinelli, 1978, p. 52, note 13, and p. 64.
86. This document, written by Sraffa, was published by Paolo Spriano in *op. cit.*, pp. 155–6; cf. also pp. 93–4.
87. Gramsci's reflections on the subject of a 'Constituent Assembly' are related in detail by Athos Lisa, *Memorie: In carcere con Gramsci*, Feltrinelli, 1973, pp. 81–103.
88. The handing over of this message was confirmed by Sraffa in a letter of 18 December 1969 to Paolo Spriano, quoted in his book, *Storia del Partito comunista italiano*, Vol. 3, *I fronti popolari, Stalin, la guerra*, Turin: Einaudi, 1970, reprinted in 1976, p. 150, note 1.
89. Tatiana Schucht: letter to P. Sraffa, 12 May 1937, published in Gramsci, *Letters from Prison*, London: Cape, 1975, Appendix, p. 277.
90. See Ambrogio Donini's letter to Sraffa of 19 May 1937 in Paolo Spriano, *Gramsci in carcere e il partito*, Riuniti, 1977, pp. 159–60. Donini was one of the persons responsible for the publications of the Italian Communist Party in Paris.
91. P. Spriano, *Gramsci in carcere e il partito*, Riuniti, 1977, p. 115.
92. See the article by Togliatti's companion, Nilde Iotti, 'Nascose ai fascisti i *Quaderni del carcere*', *Rinascita* (Rome), no 31, 3 August 1973, p. 21.
93. Togliatti: letter to P. Sraffa, 20 May 1937, published by Paolo Spriano in 'Gli ultimi anni di Gramsci in un colloquio con Piero Sraffa', *Rinascita* (Rome), no 15, 14 April 1967, p. 15.

94. Turin: Einaudi, 1967–75 (five volumes).
95. Paolo Spriano: 'L'altra metà di Gramsci', *L'Unità* (Rome) 6 September 1983, p. 3.
96. Concerning these episodes, see Giorgio Napolitano's article, 'La "vita segreta" di un grande intellettuale', *Rinascita*, no 42, 28 October 1983, p. 34.

3. FIRST YEARS IN CAMBRIDGE

1. J. M. Keynes: letter to P. Sraffa, 31 May 1927, preserved in the Keynes Papers, Marshall Library, quoted by N. Kaldor in 'Piero Sraffa (1898–1983)', *Proceedings of the British Academy*, Vol. LXXI, 1985, p. 626.
2. A. Roncaglia: *Sraffa e la teoria dei prezzi*, Laterza, 2nd edition, 1981, Appendix 'La rivoluzione di Sraffa', p. 177; A. Roncaglia: 'Piero Sraffa: una bibliografia ragionata', *Studi Economici*, 38th year, no 21, 1983, p.140.
3. Joan Robinson: 'Reminiscences', in the collection *Contributions to Modern Economics*, Oxford: Basil Blackwell, 1978, p. xi; see also Joan Robinson's preface to the French edition of *Economic Heresies* (1971): *Hérésies économiques: Essais sur quelques problèmes démodés de théorie économique*, Calmann-Lévy, 1972, pp. 7–8.
4. He was later invited to visit the Sraffa family, and, in Milan, he met Mattioli, head of the Banca Commerciale Italiana. R. F. Kahn: *The Making of Keynes' General Theory: Raffaele Mattioli Lectures*, Cambridge: Cambridge University Press, 1984, pp. 3 and 170.
5. R. F. Kahn: Preface to the Italian edition (1982) of the thesis, 'The Economics of the Short Period' (1930), *L'economia del breve periodo*, Turin: Boringhieri, 1982, pp. 36–7.
6. Joan Robinson: *The Economics of Imperfect Competition*, London: Macmillan, 1933, p. v.
7. 'Increasing Returns and the Representative Firm: A Symposium', *Economic Journal*, Vol. XL, March 1930, pp. 79–116.
8. *Ibid.*, p. 93.
9. See P. Sraffa's letter of 8 May 1930 to J. Schumpeter, preserved in the Schumpeter Papers, Harvard University Archives, Cambridge, Mass.
10. Austin Robinson: 'Keynes and his Cambridge Colleagues', in Don Patinkin and J. Clark Leith, eds., *Keynes, Cambridge and the General Theory*, London, Macmillan, 1977, p. 29.
11. Austin Robinson, lecturer in economics since 1929, had recently been appointed Secretary of the Cambridge Faculty of Economics and Politics by A. C. Pigou.
12. See J. M. Keynes: 'Mary Paley Marshall', in *Essays in Biography, The Collected Writings*, Macmillan and Cambridge University Press, Vol. X, 1972, p. 249.
13. Geoffrey C. Harcourt: 'An Early Post-Keynesian: Lorie Tarshis (or: Tarshis on Tarshis by Harcourt)', *Journal of Post-Keynesian Economics*, Vol. IV, no 4, summer 1982, p. 613.
14. London: Macmillan, 1932.
15. London: Macmillan, 1933.
16. *Economic Journal*, Vol. XLVIII, September 1938; see also J. T. Dunlop's letter of 10 May 1938 to Keynes, in J. M. Keynes, *The General Theory and After: A Supplement, The Collected Writings*, Macmillan and Cambridge University Press, Vol. XXIX, 1979, p. 285.

17. In 1821 David Ricardo had been one of the founder members of this club.
18. Brian H. Pollitt: 'The Collaboration of Maurice Dobb in Sraffa's Edition of Ricardo', *Cambridge Journal of Economics*, Vol. 12, no 1, March 1988, p. 57.
19. M. Dobb: 'Random Biographical Notes', *Cambridge Journal of Economics*, Vol. 2, no 2, June 1978, p. 117.
20. London: Routledge, 1925.
21. I learned that the two men had been in contact from a letter sent by A. Tasca to P. Sraffa (15 October 1929), which alludes to it; this letter is preserved at the Feltrinelli Foundation in Milan. Harry Pollitt had replaced Albert Inkpin, General Secretary of the party from 1920 to 1929.
22. Henri Bartoli: 'Chronique de la pensée économique en Italie', *Revue Economique*, Vol. 32, no 1, January 1981, p. 184. Keynes wrote a short essay on Ramsey, accompanied by an anthology of reflections in *Essays in Biography, The Collected Writings*, Macmillan and Cambridge University Press, Vol. X, 1972, pp. 335–46.
23. Georg Henrik von Wright: 'Biographical Sketch', in Norman Malcolm, *Ludwig Wittgenstein: A Memoir*, London: Oxford University Press, 1958, pp. 15–16.
24. Ludwig Wittgenstein, *Philosophical Investigations*, New York: Macmillan, 1958, 3rd edition, p. x (Wittgenstein's italics). As regards the relations between Sraffa and Wittgenstein, see Paolo Albani's study, 'Teoria economica e linguaggio scientifico: elementi per uno studio sul rapporto Sraffa-Wittgenstein' in *Economia Politica-Rivista di teoria e analisi* (Bologna), 1st year, no 1, April 1984, pp. 107–42; J. B. Davis, 'Sraffa, Wittgenstein and neoclassical economics', *Cambridge Journal of Economics*, vol. 12, no 1, March 1988, pp. 29–36.
25. R. F. Kahn: *The Making of Keynes' General Theory: Raffaele Mattioli Lectures*, Cambridge University Press, 1984, p. 171; A. N. L. Munby: 'The Book Collector', in Milo Keynes, ed., *Essays on John Maynard Keynes*, Cambridge University Press, 1975, pp. 290–8.
26. Joseph A. Schumpeter: *Ten Great Economists: From Marx to Keynes*, New York: Oxford University Press, 1951, pp. 272–3, note 13.
27. Cambridge: Cambridge University Press, 1938. This joint introduction was reprinted in J. M. Keynes, *Social, Political and Literary Writings, The Collected Writings*, Macmillan and Cambridge University Press, Vol. XXVIII, 1982, pp. 373–90 (Chapter 4, 'Hume').
28. J. M. Keynes: *The General Theory and after: A Supplement, The Collected Writings*, Macmillan and Cambridge University Press, Vol. XXIX, 1979, p. 3.
29. P. Sraffa: letter to Tatiana Schucht, 9 September 1931. In *Nuove lettere di Antonio Gramsci con altre lettere di Piero Sraffa*, Rome: Riuniti, 1986, pp. 69–70.
30. See J. M. Keynes: *A Treatise on Money*, Vol. 1, Chapter 18 ('Changes due to Investment Factors'), and Vol. II, Chapter 37 ('Methods of National Management', III, 'The Control of the Rate of Investment', paragraph IV, 'The Slump of 1930') in *The Collected Writings*, Macmillan and Cambridge University Press, 1971, resp. Vol. V, pp. 248–62, and Vol. VI, pp. 338–47.
31. See J. M. Keynes: *Activities 1929–1931: Rethinking Employment and Unemployment Policies, The Collected Writings*, Vol. XX, Macmillan and Cambridge University Press, 1981, resp. pp. 72–5 and 128–40.
32. See J. M. Keynes: *The General Theory and after*, Part I, *Preparation, The*

Collected Writings, Vol. XIII, Macmillan and Cambridge University Press, 1973, p. 83.

33. Joan Robinson: 'Reminiscences' (1977) in *Contributions to Modern Economics*, Basil Blackwell, 1978, p. xii.
34. At the time, Keynes was in London during the week, and spent long weekends in Cambridge.
35. About the organization of the 'Circus', see Donald Moggridge, 'The Cambridge Circus: 1930–1931', in J. M. Keynes, *The General Theory and after*: Part I, *Preparation, The Collected Writings*, Vol. XIII, Macmillan and Cambridge University Press, 1973, pp. 337–43. About the subjects discussed, see Joan Robinson: 'Reminiscences' (1977), in *Contributions to Modern Economics*, Basil Blackwell, 1978, p. xii-xv, and R. F. Kahn: *The Making of Keynes' General Theory: Raffaele Mattioli Lectures*, Cambridge: Cambridge University Press, 1984, pp. 106–9.
36. Letter published in J. M. Keynes, *The General Theory and after*: Part I, *Preparation, The Collected Writings*, Vol. XIII, Macmillan and Cambridge University Press, 1973, pp. 207–9. Keynes answered on 15 May 1931, in *op. cit.*, pp. 209–11.
37. Austin Robinson: 'Keynes and his Cambridge Colleagues', in Don Patinkin and J. Clark Leith, eds., *Keynes, Cambridge and the General Theory*, Macmillan, 1977, p. 29.
38. See Hans Staehle: 'La réunion de la Société d'économétrie, Lausanne, septembre 1931', *Econometrica*, Vol. 1, 1933, pp. 73 and 79. Henry E. Lloyd, who drew his ideas from mercantilism and was a great friend of Pietro Verri, suggested an algebraic formulation for the equation of the quantitative theory of money in *An Essay on the Theory of Money*, published anonymously in London in 1771. Sraffa had been elected Fellow of the recently Econometric Society, in the Italian section.
39. L. Tarshis: 'Keynes as Seen by his Students in the thirties', in Don Patinkin and J. Clark Leith, eds., *op. cit.*, p. 52.
40. Austin Robinson, 'Discussion', in Don Patinkin and J. Clark Leith, eds., *op. cit.*, p. 88.
41. As regards these years, there exist an undated letter from Sraffa to Keynes and two undated letters from Keynes to Sraffa, published in J. M. Keynes: *The General Theory and after: A Supplement, The Collected Writings*, Vol. XXIX, Macmillan and Cambridge University Press, 1979, resp. pp. 157 and 158–60.
42. J. M. Keynes: letter to Lydia Keynes, 3 December 1933, Keynes Papers, King's College, Cambridge, quoted by R. Skidelsky, 'Keynes and Sraffa: a problem of non-communication', Italian translation, 'Keynes e Sraffa: un caso di non-communicazione', in R. Bellofiore, ed., *Tra teoria economica e grande cultura europea: Piero Sraffa*, Milan: Franco Angeli, 1986, p. 78. See also Keynes: *The General Theory and after: A Supplement, The Collected Writings*, Vol. XXIX, *op. cit.*, p. 62.
43. An extract from this letter, preserved among the Keynes Papers, King's College, Cambridge, was published by R. Skidelsky in *op. cit.*, p. 78.
44. In 1938, Celestino Arena made the suggestion that Sraffa should translate the *General Theory* into Italian as part of a projected 'Nuova collana di economisti' in the 'Biblioteca dell' Economista'. Sraffa answered: '... I am unfortunately immersed at the moment in an edition of Ricardo, and as long as it remains unfinished, I cannot take on any other engagements'. P. Sraffa: letter to Celestino

Arena, 12 August 1938, published by Alberto Zanni, 'Sulla mancata apparizione della 'Teoria generale' di Keynes in una seconda serie della 'Nuova collana di economisti' (con corrispondenze inediti)', *Quaderni di storia dell'economia politica*, 3rd year, no 3, 1985, p. 266. In this letter Sraffa said that he had been given the author's permission to publish an Italian translation of the *General Theory* in the series, and that he was ready to collaborate in an (unspecified) 'choice of polemical writings' by Keynes, which were to be part of the same volume. These projects did not in fact come to fruition, and the Italian translation by Alberto Campolongo only came out in 1947.

45. D. H. Robertson: 'Some Notes on Mr Keynes' General Theory of Employment', *Quarterly Journal of Economics*, Vol. LI, November 1936, p. 168; *Essays in Monetary Theory*, London: King and Son, 1940, preface, p. viii.
46. F. A. von Hayek: 'Reflections on the Pure Theory of Money of Mr J. M. Keynes', *Economica*, Vol. XI, no 33, August 1931, pp. 270–95. The second part of the study appeared in *Economica*, Vol. XII, no 35, February 1932, pp. 22–44.
47. J. M. Keynes: 'The Pure Theory of Money: A Reply to Dr Hayek', *Economica*, Vol. xi, no 34, November 1931, p. 394, republished in *The General Theory and after:* Part I, *Preparation, The Collected Writings*, Macmillan and Cambridge University Press, Vol. XIII, 1973, p. 252. F. von Hayek wrote 'A Rejoinder to Mr Keynes', published in *Economica* (Vol. XI, no 34, November 1931, pp. 398–403), in which he takes Keynes to task for not having answered his criticisms and for having been too hasty in condemning *Prices and Production*.
48. P. Sraffa: 'Dr Hayek on Money and Capital', *Economic Journal*, Vol. XLII, March 1932, pp. 42–53.
49. *Ibid*., p. 43.
50. See J. M. Keynes: *The General Theory of Employment, Interest and Money*, chapter 17, 'The Essential Properties of Interest and Money', *The Collected Writings*, Vol. VII, Macmillan and Cambridge University Press, 1973, p. 222–44. This deals with the Keynesian concept of 'own rate of interest'.
51. F. A. von Hayek: 'Money and Capital: A Reply', *Economic Journal*, Vol. XLII, June 1932, pp. 237–49.
52. *Ibid*., p. 249.
53. P. Sraffa: 'A Rejoinder', *Economic Journal*, Vol. XLII, June 1932, pp. 249–51.
54. A Tasca: 'La rivalutazione della lira e la crisi della economia italiana', *Lo Stato Operaio*, 1st year, no 6, August 1927, p. 667.
55. Sraffa's italics. P. Sraffa and A. Tasca: 'Il vero significato della "quota 90"', in Lucio Villari, ed., *Il capitalismo italiano del Novecento*, Vol. I, Bari: Laterza, 1975, pp. 180–1. I was able, while reading the Sraffa-Tasca correspondence at the Feltrinelli Foundation in Milan, to find the dates of the various letters in question.
56. P. Togliatti: *Lezioni sul fascismo*, Rome: Riuniti, 1970.
57. *Op cit.*, pp. 182–5. See also the 'Postscript', consisting in fact of an extract from a letter from A. Tasca to P. Sraffa of 5 October 1927.
58. *Ibid*., p. 186.
59. *Ibid*., p. 189.
60. A. Tasca: letter to P. Sraffa, 9 November 1927, preserved at the Feltrinelli Foundation in Milan.
61. P. Sraffa: letter to A. Tasca, 21 December 1927, preserved at the Feltrinelli Foundation in Milan. In this he said that he was sorry to have taken so long in giving his consent.

62. *Lo Stato Operaio*, 1st year, no 9–10, pp. 1089–95.
63. Cf. a letter from P. Sraffa to A. Tasca, undated but most probably from the summer of 1930, marked 'Cambridge, domenica', preserved at the Feltrinelli Foundation in Milan.
64. It will be noted that Tasca published the study by David Riazanov, 'Antonio Labriola', in *Lo Stato Operaio*, no 7, September 1927, pp. 787–92.
65. On Labriola's Marxism, see Jean-Pierre Potier, *Lectures italiennes de Marx: Les conflits d'interprétation chez les économistes et les philosophes, 1883–1983*, Lyon: Presses Universitaires de Lyon, 1986, pp. 131–54.
66. Rome: Loescher, 1895.
67. Rome: Loescher, 1896.
68. Rome: Loescher, 1897.
69. As appears from the letter from A. Tasca to P. Sraffa of 21 October 1927, preserved at the Feltrinelli Foundation in Milan.
70. A. Tasca: letter to P. Sraffa, 9 November 1927, preserved at the Feltrinelli Foundation in Milan.
71. *Lo Stato Operaio*, 1st year, 1927, no 7, September, no 8, October, no 9–10, November–December; 2nd year, 1928, no 1–2, January–February, no 3, March, no 4, April, no 5, May, no 6, June, no 7, July, no 8, August–September, no 9, October; 3rd year, 1929, no 1, January, no 2, February, no 4, April–May, no 6, July–August, no 7, September–October, no 8, November; 4th year, 1930, no 1, January, no 2, February.
72. A. Tasca: letter to P. Sraffa, 9 November 1927, preserved at the Feltrinelli Foundation in Milan.
73. Both these letters from Labriola were published in the collection of Labriola's work, *Scritti filosofici e politici*, Franco Sbarberi, ed., Turin: Einaudi, 1973, Vol. I, resp. pp. 320–5 and 403–6.
74. P. Sraffa: letters to A. Tasca, 21 December 1927 and 13 March 1928, preserved at the Feltrinelli Foundation in Milan.
75. *Lo Stato Operaio*, 3rd year, no 2, February 1929, p. 154, note 1.
76. *Lo Stato Operaio*, 3rd year, no 7, September–October 1929, p. 622, note 1.
77. P. Sraffa: letter to A. Tasca, 24 February 1928, preserved at the Feltrinelli Foundation in Milan. Tasca's presentation is in the no 7, September 1927 edition of *Lo Stato Operaio*, pp. 795–6, between Riazanov's article and the first series of letters.
78. B. Croce: 'Note sulla letteratura italiana nella seconda metà del secolo XIX, 23, Giovanni Bovio e la poesia della filosofia', Parte seconda, 'Antonio Labriola—Giovanni Bovio', paragraph VII, 'Antonio Labriola', *La Critica* (Naples), 5th year, fasc. VI, 20 November 1907, pp. 417–21; B. Croce: 'Appunti per la storia della cultura in Italia nella seconda metà del secolo XIX', 1, 'La vita letteraria a Napoli dal 1860 al 1900', Prima parte, *La Critica*, 7th year, fasc. 5, 1909, p. 334 and ff.
79. About the activities of Mattioli during the thirties, see Giovanni Malagodi's book, *Profilo di Raffaele Mattioli*, Milan: Riccardo Ricciardi, ed., 1984.
80. Mattioli was thanked by Sraffa in the 'General Preface', *The Works and Correspondence of David Ricardo*, Cambridge: Cambridge University Press, 1951, p. xi.
81. The Italian translation by Enrico Radaeli was published in 1932–34.
82. About this book, see above, pp.31–2.
83. See the letters from R. Morandi to Pietro Ernandez, 22 May and 27 August 1932,

in *Annali della Fondazione Einaudi* (Turin), Vol. III, 1969, resp. pp. 464 and 467.
84. London: Methuen, 1st edition, 1904, 4th edition, 1925.
85. R. Morandi: letter to P. Ernandez, 10 March 1934, in *Annali della Fondazione Einaudi*, Vol. III, 1969, p. 479.
86. Secretary of the reconstituted Italian Socialist Party from December 1945 to April 1946, he was, in 1946–47, Minister of Industry and Commerce in De Gasperi's government. He was one of the intellectual mentors of the founder of Italian 'operaïsmo', Raniero Panzieri. Cf. Jean-Pierre Potier: *Lectures italiennes de Marx, 1883–1983*, Lyon: Presses Universitaires de Lyon, 1986, pp. 401–23.
87. J. M. Keynes: *Activities 1939–45: Internal War Finance, The Collected Writings*, Vol. XXII, Macmillan and Cambridge University Press, 1978, pp. 190–1.
88. Charles H. Hession: *John Maynard Keynes*, New York: Macmillan, 1983, p.382. After her husband's death, in 1938, Irma Sraffa went to live with her son in Cambridge. She died in 1945.
89. N Kaldor: *Ricordi di un economista*, Milan: Garzanti, 1986, p. 68.
90. N. Kaldor revealed an amusing anecdote about this: Sraffa was hoping to soften Pigou by offering him a jar of orange marmalade which he had bought after saving his ration coupons for several weeks, in *op. cit.*, pp. 49–50.

4. THE PUBLICATION OF RICARDO'S *COLLECTED WORKS* AND *PRODUCTION OF COMMODITIES BY MEANS OF COMMODITIES*

1. Underlined in the original, letter from J. M. Keynes to Lydia Keynes, 28 November 1927, Keynes Papers, King's College, Cambridge, quoted by Robert Skidelsky in 'Keynes e Sraffa: un caso di non-communicazione', R. Bellofiore, ed. *Tra teoria economica e grande cultura europea: Piero Sraffa*, Milan: Franco Angeli, 1986, p. 77.
2. Sraffa's italics. *Production of Commodities by Means of Commodities*, 'Preface', Cambridge University Press, 1960, p. vi.
3. A. S. Besicovitch, of Trinity College, apparently helped Sraffa with the second part of the book, 'Multiple-product Industries and Fixed Capital'.
4. *The Works of David Ricardo*, with a notice of the life and writings of the author by J. R. McCulloch, London: J. Murray, 1846.
5. *Economic Journal*, Vol. XL, December 1930, p. 710.
6. L. Einaudi: 'Per una nuova collana di economisti', *La Riforma Sociale*, 38th year, Vol. XLII, no 7–8, July–August 1931, p. 397.
7. A. Gramsci: letter to Tatiana Schucht, 7 September 1931, in *Gramsci's Prison Letters: Lettere dal Carcere*, London: Zwan, 1988, p. 161.
8. Turin, UTET, 1925.
9. Paris: Sirey, 5th edition, 1926.
10. P. Sraffa: letter to Tatiana Schucht, 2 October 1931, in *Nuove lettere di Antonio Gramsci con altre lettere di Piero Sraffa*, Riuniti, 1986, p. 71.
11. P. Sraffa: letter to J. M. Keynes, 23 March 1930, Keynes Papers, quoted by Pier Luigi Porta in 'How Piero Sraffa Took up the Editorship of Ricardo's *Works and Correspondence*', *The History of Economics Society Bulletin*, Vol. VIII, no 1, summer 1986, p. 35.

12. Grandson of David, second son of the economist.
13. Grandson of Mortimer, third son of the economist.
14. J. M. Keynes: letter to Lydia Keynes, 1 June 1930, Keynes Papers, King's College, Cambridge, quoted by R. Skidelsky in 'Keynes e Sraffa: un caso di non-communicazione', R. Bellofiore, ed., *Tra teoria economica e grande cultura europea: Piero Sraffa*, Milan: Franco Angeli, 1986, p. 79.
15. P. Sraffa: letter to L. Einaudi, 5 June 1930, preserved at the Luigi Einaudi Foundation in Turin. André Liesse (1854–1944) was Professor of Economics at the Ecole Spéciale d'Architecture in Paris, at the Conservatoire National des Arts et Métiers and at the Ecole Libre des Sciences Politiques; author of *Vauban économiste* (1891) and of *La statistique, ses difficultés, ses procédés, ses résultats* (1905).
16. See the conversation between P. Sraffa and Arnold Heertje, related by the latter in 'On discovering a second "freak" copy of Ricardo's *Principles* and the Say Archives', *History of Economics Society Bulletin*, Vol. 10, no 1, spring 1988, p. 76.
17. P. Sraffa: 'A Survey of Ricardo Manuscripts', Appendix B, in *Biographical Miscellany, The Works and Correspondence of David Ricardo*, Vol. X, Cambridge University Press, 1955, p. 387.
18. L. Einaudi: 'Come non si devono ristampare i nostri classici', *Rivista di Storia Economica* (Turin), 1st year, no 1, March 1936, pp. 75–80.
19. 'An Alleged Correction of Ricardo', *Quarterly Journal of Economics*, Vol. XLIV, May 1930, pp. 539–44 (Sraffa), p. 545 (Einaudi).
20. P. Sraffa: 'Addenda to the Memoir of Ricardo', in *Biographical Miscellany, The Works and Correspondence of David Ricardo*, Vol. X, Cambridge University Press, 1955, p. 18, note 3.
21. Huguette Biaujeaud: *Essai sur la théorie ricardienne de la valeur*, Paris: Sirey, 1934, reprinted Paris: Economica, 1988, p. 18, note 1. This doctoral thesis, supervised by Gaëtan Pirou, was defended in December 1933 at the University of Paris. Sraffa asked H. Biaujeaud to help him search, in France, for the letters from Ricardo to James Mill, but without result (*op. cit.* , p. 113). These letters were found in 1943 (see below).
22. See P. Sraffa: 'Addenda to the Memoir of Ricardo' and 'Ricardo in Business', in *Biographical Miscellany, The Works and Correspondence of David Ricardo*, Vol. X, Cambridge University Press, 1955, resp. pp. 16–64 and pp. 65–106.
23. J. M. Keynes: 'Thomas Robert Malthus', in *Essays in Biography, The Collected Writings*, Vol. X, Macmillan and Cambridge University Press, 1972, p. 97.
24. See the letter from R. Morandi to P. Ernandez of 10 March 1934, already quoted, p.57, note 85.
25. The date was in fact 1923, and not 1922.
26. See note 28.
27. A. Gramsci: letter to Tatiana Schucht, 30 May 1932, in *Gramsci's Prison Letters: Lettere dal Carcere*, London: Zwan, 1988, p. 219–20.
28. In fact, Gramsci's attribution to Ricardo of the paternity of the concept of 'determinate market' was unjustified, since he had found it in the work of the Italian marginalist economist Pasquale Jannaccone, in a completely different context: '... in economic science, the expressions free competition and monopoly are only two formulae that indicate in a synthetic way that the fulfilment of a certain number of conditions makes the market *determinate*, while the absence of one of them makes it *indeterminate*. The fundamental problem of economics

being the determination of ratios of exchange (values, prices), it is evident that economists attach maximum importance to states of perfect free competition and absolute monopoly, because only under one of these two hypotheses will there be a determinate situation of stable equilibrium, and, therefore, a normal price to which the real market prices will converge, just as satellites revolve around their sun' (italics in original), 'Scienza, critica e realtà economica', *La Riforma Sociale*, 37th year, Vol. XLI, no 11–12, November–December 1930, p. 524; see also Jean-Pierre Potier: *Lectures italiennes de Marx: Les conflits d'interprétation chez les économistes et les philosophes, 1883–1983*, Lyon: Presses Universitaires de Lyon, 1986, pp. 223 and ff.

29. *Ibid*, p. 221.
30. P. Sraffa: letter to Tatiana Schucht, 21 June 1932, preserved at the Gramsci Foundation in Rome. This extract, in the version sent by Tatiana Schucht to Gramsci on 5 July 1932, was published by Nicolà Badaloni in his study 'Gramsci: la filosofia della prassi come previsione', in the collection *Storia del Marxismo*, Vol. 3, *Il marxismo nell' età della Terza Internazionale*, Part 2, 'Dalla crisi del' 29 al XX Congresso', Turin: Einaudi, 1981, p. 296.
31. Alfred Marshall: *Principles of Economics*, 8th edition (1920), London: Macmillan, reprinted 1959, pp. 27–8.
32. P. Sraffa: quoted letter of 21 June 1932, preserved at the Gramsci Foundation in Rome.
33. Leipzig: Kröner, 1932, two volumes.
34. The first German edition of the 'Critique of Hegel's Philosophy of Law', published in 1927 in the first volume of the *Marx-Engels Gesamtausgabe* (Marx-Engels Archiv Verlag: Frankfurt am Main), was the work of the Marx-Engels Institute of Moscow, under the direction of David Riazanov. Gramsci heard of the existence of this text in a review published by B. Croce in his journal *La Critica* in 1930 (see *Quaderni del Carcere*, Einaudi, 1975, Notebook 10, p. 1240).
35. S. Landhut and J. P. Mayer published in their collection the first German edition of the 'Economic and Philosophic Manuscripts of 1844', but the text was incomplete and the title incorrect. The integral version was published a few months later, the same year (1932), in the third volume of the *Marx-Engels Gesamtausgabe* (Berlin), edited by the Marx-Engels Institute of Moscow, this time under the direction of V. Adoratski.
36. Brian H. Pollitt: 'The Collaboration of Maurice Dobb in Sraffa's edition of Ricardo', *Cambridge Journal of Economics*, Vol. 12, no 1, March 1988, p. 59.
37. This correspondence was published by George O'Brien in 'J. S. Mill and J. E. Cairnes', *Economica* (London), Vol. X, no 40, November 1943, pp. 273–85.
38. P. Sraffa: letter to J. M. Keynes, 5 July 1943, Keynes Papers. An extract from this report was quoted by J. M. Keynes in a letter to Jacob Viner of 17 October 1943, in *Activities, 1940–1944: Shaping the Post-war World: The Clearing Union, The Collected Writings*, Vol. XXV, Cambridge University Press, 1980, p. 335.
39. Brian H. Pollitt: 'The Collaboration of Maurice Dobb in Sraffa's edition of Ricardo', *Cambridge Journal of Economics*, Vol. 12, no 1, March 1988, pp. 56 and 60–2.
40. Sraffa and his friends stayed near the 'Passo Sella' (2240 m), not far from the village of Canazei, in the Italian Dolomites. R. F. Kahn recalled that holiday: 'It was early in the summer and there was too much snow. Our rock climbing was

restricted. Roy Harrod's book *Towards a Dynamic Economics* was in page proof and Harrod lent me a proof, which we read when we were not walking or climbing' (R. F. Kahn: *The Making of Keynes' General Theory: Raffaele Mattioli Lectures*, Cambridge University Press, 1984, p. 4). In the summer of 1951, Sraffa again went to the mountains, this time in Austria, with his friends R. F. Kahn, J. Robinson and N. Kaldor, as is shown by a letter from P. Sraffa to L. Einaudi dated 18 August 1951, preserved at the Einaudi Foundation in Turin.

41. Maurice Dobb Archives, quoted by Brian H. Pollitt: 'The Collaboration of Maurice Dobb in Sraffa's edition of Ricardo', *Cambridge Journal of Economics*, Vol. 12, no 1, March 1988, p.63.
42. Einaudi had first been Governor of the Bank of Italy (1945–1947), then Vice-President of the Council and Minister of the Budget in the government of Alcide De Gasperi (May 1947–May 1948).
43. 'Dalla leggenda al monumento', *Giornale degli Economisti e Annali di Economia*, 10th year, new series, no 7–8, July–August 1951, pp. 329–34.
44. Letter from P. Sraffa to L. Einaudi of 6 September 1951, preserved at the Einaudi Foundation in Turin.
45. *Economic Journal*, Vol. LXV, September 1955, pp. 543–4, later reprinted in Vol. XI of Ricardo's *Works: General Index*, Cambridge University Press, 1973.
46. A photograph of this letter from P. Sraffa to G. Einaudi of 30 October 1948 was published in the volume *Cinquant' anni di un editore: Le Edizioni Einaudi negli anni 1933–1983*, Turin: Einaudi, 1983.
47. The liberal Francesco Ferrara (1810–1900) launched the series and directed it until 1868; it contained the great works of political economy which had been written since the eighteenth century. The task was then carried on by Gerolamo Boccardo, Salvatore Cognetti de Martiis, Pasquale Jannaccone, Giuseppe Bottai and Celestino Arena.
48. L. Einaudi: *Saggi bibliografici e storici intorno alle dottrine economiche*, Rome: Edizioni di Storia e Letteratura, 1953 (chapt 1, 'Francesco Ferrara I: Viaggio tra i miei libri', p. 5).
49. R. Cantillon: *Saggio sulla natura del commercio in generale*, Sergio Cotta and Antonio Giolitti, eds., introduction by L. Einaudi ('Che cosa ha detto Cantillon?'), 1955, reprinted Einaudi, 1974. The translation was based on the edition by H. Higgs (London, 1931) and took into account the INED (Institut National d'Etudes Démographiques) edition, Paris 1952.
50. Paris: INED, 1958, two volumes .
51. Leyden and Paris, 1767–68, two volumes. Letter from P. Sraffa to L. Einaudi of 22 August 1958, four typed pages, preserved at the Luigi Einaudi Foundation in Turin, published in *Political Economy: Studies in the Surplus Approach*, Vol. 4, no 1, 1988, pp. 153–5.
52. R. L. Meek defended his doctoral thesis in 1949, 'The Development of the Concept of Surplus in Economic Thought from Mun to Mill'.
53. Graham S. L. Tucker published his doctoral thesis with the title *Progress and Profits in British Economic Thought, 1650–1850*, Cambridge: Cambridge University Press, 1960.
54. P. Garegnani defended his doctoral thesis in 1958, *A Problem in the Theory of Distribution from Ricardo to Wicksell* (1958), which led to *Il capitale nelle teorie della distribuzione*, Milan: Giuffrè, 1960.
55. This was a letter, dated 17 February 1877, from Léon Walras to Charles Letort thanking him for an article (which in fact did no more than mention his name),

'De l'application des mathématiques à l'étude de l'économie politique', published in *L'Economiste français*, Vol. 3, 2nd year, 31 October 1874. See *Correspondence of Léon Walras and Related Papers*, William Jaffé, ed., Amsterdam: North Holland, Vol. 1, 1965, pp. 528–9, letter no 373.

56. 'Lo sviluppo del commercio cino-britannico: 1952–55', in *Bollettino del Centro Studi per lo Sviluppo delle Relazioni Economiche e Culturali con la Cina*, no 4, June 1955, pp. 14–18: article discovered by Sergio Steve.
57. P. Sraffa: Preface to the *Production of Commodities by Means of Commodities*, Cambridge University Press, 1960, p. vi.
58. The publishers were, respectively, Cambridge University Press and G. Einaudi. Sraffa presented a specially bound copy to L. Einaudi; see P. Sraffa: letter to L. Einaudi, dated 20 May 1960, preserved at the Einaudi Foundation in Turin. In this letter we learn that L. Einaudi had sent Sraffa a collection of articles, *Cronache economiche e politiche di un trentennio (1893–1925)*, Vol. 3 (1910–1914), Einaudi: Turin, 1960. In January, he had already sent him Vol. 2 (1903–1909), Einaudi, 1959; Sraffa thanked him for the book, saying he had found it 'una delizia', and promising to give it a careful reading (see Sraffa's letter of 17 January 1960 to L. Einaudi, preserved at the Einaudi Foundation in Turin).
59. See for example M. W. Reder, 'Review of *Production of Commodities by Means of Commodities* by P. Sraffa', *American Economic Review*, Vol. LI, September 1961, pp. 688–95; R. E. Quandt, 'Review of *Production of Commodities by Means of Commodities* by P. Sraffa', *Journal of Political Economy*, Vol. LXIX, October 1961, p. 500.
60. Roy F. Harrod: 'Review of *Production of Commodities by Means of Commodities*', *Economic Journal*, Vol. LXXI, December 1961, pp. 783–7.
61. Piero Sraffa: *Production of Commodities*: A Comment', *Economic Journal*, Vol. LXXII, June 1962, pp. 477–9.
62. Peter K. Newman: 'Production of Commodities by Means of Commodities', *Schweizerische Zeitschrift für Volkswirtschaft und Statistik: Revue suisse d'économie politique et de statistique*, Vol. XCVIII, March 1962, p. 59.
63. P. K. Newman wrote again on 8 June and Sraffa on 19 June 1962. In 1970 the three letters were published by Krishna Bharadwaj in an appendix to his article, 'On the Maximum Number of Switches between two Production Systems', in *Schweizerische Zeitschrift für Volkswirtschaft und Statistik: Revue suisse d'économie politique et de statistique*, Vol. CVI, December 1970, pp. 425–8.
64. Joan Robinson: 'Prelude to a Critique of Economic Theory', *Oxford Economic Papers*, Vol. XIII, February 1961, pp. 57–8.
65. Claudio Napoleoni: 'Sulla teoria della produzione come processo circolare', *Giornale degli Economisti e Annali di Economia* (Padua), Vol. XX, January–February 1961, pp. 101–17.
66. R. L. Meek: 'Mr Sraffa's Rehabilitation of Classical Economics', *Scottish Journal of Political Economy*, Vol. VIII, June 1961, reprinted in *Economics and Ideology and other Essays: Studies in the Development of Economic Thought*, London: Chapman and Hall, 1967, p. 177.
67. M. Dobb: 'An Epoch-making Book', *The Labour Monthly* (London), October 1961, pp. 487–91.
68. This account is presented by Gilles Dostaler in 'Marx et Sraffa', the enlarged version of a paper read at the 'Keynes and Sraffa' symposium organized by the

University of Ottawa on 13 March 1981, and was published in *L'Actualité Economique* (Montreal), no 1–2, January–June 1982, pp. 102–3.

69. J. K. Whitaker: 'Acknowledgements', in *The Early Economic Writings of Alfred Marshall: 1867–1890*, edited and introduced by J. K. Whitaker, Vol. I, London: Macmillan, 1975, p. xi.
70. Luca Meldolesi: 'Piero Sraffa, il percorso di un' analisi e di una cultura e vicenda morale e mentale di un comunista degli anni '20, da Marx a Ricardo (e St Simon)', *Il Manifesto* (Rome), 6 June 1980, p.3, and Luca Meldolesi, preface to *L'utopia realmente esistente: Marx e Saint-Simon*, Bari: Laterza, 1982, p. viii.
71. This volume was only published in 1973.
72. Little weight should be given to Maria-Antonietta Macciocchi's account of a visit to Sraffa in May 1973 which she gave in the postscript 'Paris-Cambridge-Paris' of her book *Per Gramsci*, Bologna: Il Mulino, 1974. Though she attempts to convey the atmosphere of the place, her portrait of the great economist is very cruel and unjust.
73. A. Roncaglia: 'In redazione o in pizzeria', in *Cento anni Laterza, 1885–1985: Testimonianze degli autori*, Bari: Laterza, 1985, p. 213.
74. Aurelio Macchioro: 'A proposito di una collana ISEDI di classici del pensiero economico', *Storia del Pensiero Economico: Bollettino di Informazione* (Florence), no 1, March 1973, p. 17.
75. P. Sraffa, *Saggi*, Bologna: Il Mulino, 1986. The series was sponsored by the Istituto Bancario San Paolo of Turin. In France, the two articles of 1925 and 1926 as well as the Introduction to the *Works and correspondence* of David Ricardo, were published in 1975 in one volume, G. Faccarello, ed. *Ecrits d'économie politique*, by Economica in Paris.
76. N. Kaldor: 'Piero Sraffa (1898–1983)', *Proceedings of the British Academy*, Vol. LXXI, 1985, p. 627, note 2.
77. At a ceremony organized in his honour, a message by the Italian President, Sandro Pertini, was read out. It sums up quite well the sort of man Piero Sraffa was: 'He was the genial heir and innovator of a great tradition of economic thought, an illustrious teacher to generations of scholars, a pinnacle of democratic and anti-fascist European culture, an active supporter of the struggle for the development of democratic civilization. A great Italian has died, an Italian in whom the spirit of enquiry and the highest moral and political conscience were combined.' *Cambridge Journal of Economics*, Vol. 8, no 1, March 1984, p. 1.

POSTSCRIPT

1. I here adopt Donald A. Walker's useful taxonomy, in 'Biography and the study of the history of economic thought', in Warren J. Samuels, ed., *Research in the History of Economic Thought and Methodology*, Vol. 1, *The Craft of the Historian of Economic Thought*, Greenwich, Conn.: Jai Press, 1983, p. 47 and ff.

Bibliography

Aijado, Manuel, 'Piero Sraffa: notas para una biografia intelectual', *Cuadernos de Economia Aplicada*, Centro de Estudios Universitarios Ramón Areces (Madrid), 1985.

Albani, Paolo, 'Teoria economica e linguaggio scientifico: elementi per uno studio sul rapporto Sraffa-Wittgenstein', *Economia Politica* (Bologna), 1st year, No. 1, April 1984, pp. 107–42.

Amendola, Giógio, 'Gramsci-Togliatti, negli anni della Svolta', *Rinascita Sarda*, March 1967, reprinted as 'Le lettere di Gramsci', in G. Amendola, *Comunismo, anti-fascismo, resistenza*, Rome: Riuniti, 1967, pp. 433–7.

—— *Un' isola*, Milan: Rizzoli, 1980. French translation, *L'île: Mémoires d'un exil*, Paris: Liana Levi & Sylvie Messinger, 1983.

Badaloni, Nicolà, 'Gramsci: la filosofia della prassi come previsione', in the collection *Storia del marxismo*, Vol. 3, *Il marxismo nell' età della Terza Internazionale*, Part 2, *Dalla crisi del' 29 al XX Congresso*, Turin: Einaudi, 1981, pp. 251–340.

Bartoli, Henri, 'Chronique de la pensée économique en Italie', *Revue Économique*, vol. 32, No. 1, January 1981, pp. 180–7.

Bellofiore, Riccardo (ed.) *Tra teoria economica e grande cultura europea: Piero Sraffa*, Milan: Franco Angeli, 1986.

Berenson, Mary, letter to John Maynard Keynes, 15 June 1921, Keynes Papers, Marshall Library, Cambridge, published in *Keynes in Italia: Catalogo bibliografico*, ed. Facoltà di Economia e Commercio, Università di Firenze, Banca Toscana Studi e Informazioni (Florence), No. 7, 1983, p. 163.

Bergami, Giancarlo, *Il giovane Gramsci e il marxismo, 1911–18*, Milan: Feltrinelli, 1977.

Biaujeaud, Huguette, *Essai sur la théorie ricardienne de la valeur*, thesis, Université de Paris, Decembre 1933, Paris: Sirey, 1934, reprinted with an 'Avant-propos' by Gilbert Abraham-Frois, Paris: Economica, 1988.

Davis, J. B., 'Sraffa, Wittgenstein and Neoclassical Economics', *Cambridge Journal of Economics*, vol. 12, No. 1, March 1988, pp. 29–36.

De Felice, Franco, 'Nord e Sud nel pensiero di Rodolfo Morandi: dalla *Storia della grande industria* alla Resistenza', *Rivista Storica del Socialismo* (Milan), 7th year, No. 21, January–April 1964, pp. 21–67.

De Grand, Alexander J., *Angelo Tasca: Un politico scomodo*, Milan: Franco Angeli, 1985.

Dobb, Maurice: 'An Epoch-making Book' [review of *Production of Commodities by means of Commodities*], *Labour Monthly* (London), October 1961, pp. 487–91.

—— 'Random Biographical Notes', *Cambridge Journal of Economics*, Vol. 2, No. 2, June 1978, pp. 115–20.

Dostaler, Gilles: 'Marx et Sraffa', *L'Actualité Economique* (Montreal), No. 1–2, January–June 1982, pp. 95–114.

Eatwell, John: 'Rivoluzionò la storia delle idee' (read on the occasion of a remembrance ceremony, Rome, 25 October 1983), *Rinascita* (Rome), No. 42, 28 October 1983, pp. 33–5.

—— and Panico, Carlo: 'Sraffa, Piero (1898–1983)', in *The New Palgrave: A Dictionary of Economics*, ed. John Eatwell, Murray Milgate and Peter Newman, London: Macmillan, Vol. IV, 1987, pp. 445–52.

Einaudi, Luigi: 'Per una nuova collana di economisti', *La Riforma Sociale* (Turin), 38th year, Vol. XLII, No. 7–8, July–August 1931, pp. 394–9.

—— 'Dalla leggenda al monumento' (review of the first two volumes of *The Works and Correspondence* of D. Ricardo), *Giornale degli Economisti e Annali di Economia* (Padua), 10th year, new series, No. 7–8, July–August 1951, pp. 329–34.

—— *Saggi bibliografici e storici intorno alle dottrine economiche*, Rome: Edizioni di Storia e Letteratura, 1953.

Enciclopedia italiana di scienze, lettere ed arte, art. 'Sraffa, Angelo', Vol. XXXII, Rome: Istituto della Enciclopedia Italiana, fondata da Giovanni Treccani, 1931, p. 430.

Faucci, Riccardo: 'Fra Einaudi e Gramsci: Sraffa e la cultura economica italiana degli anni Venti', in Riccardo Bellofiore, ed., *Tra teoria economica e grande cultura europea: Piero Sraffa*, Milan: Franco Angeli, 1986, pp. 19–37.

Ferreri, Dino: 'Come si è formato l'edizione critica [of *Quaderni del Carcere* by Gramsci], *Rinascita* (Rome), No. 30, 25 July 1975, pp. 14–15.

Gattei, Giorgio: 'In merito ad un possibile rapporto tra Sraffa e Graziadei', in Roberto Finzi, ed.: *Neo-ricardiana: Sraffa e Graziadei*, Bologna: Il Mulino, 1977, pp. 211–18.

Gerratana, Valentino: 'Note di filologia gramsciana', *Studi Storici* (Rome), 16th year, No. 1, January–March 1975, pp. 126–54.

Gramsci, Antonio: *L'Ordine Nuovo, 1919–1920*, ed. V. Gerratana and A. A. Santucci, Turin: Einaudi, 1987 .

—— *La costruzione del Partito Comunista, 1923–1926*, Turin: Einaudi, 1971.

—— *La questione meridionale*, ed. F. De Felice and V. Parlato, Rome: Riuniti, 1966.

—— *Quaderni del Carcere*, ed. Valentino Gerratana, Turin: Einaudi, 1975, 4 vols.

—— *Lettere dal carcere*, ed. Sergio Caprioglio and Elsa Fubini, Turin: Einaudi, 1965.

—— *Letters from Prison, trans. and ed. Lynne Lawner*, London: Jonathan Cape, 1975.

—— *Gramsci's Prison Letters – Lettere dal Carcere: A selection, trans. Hamish Henderson*, London: Zwan Publications in association with Edinburgh Review, 1988.

—— *Nuove lettere di Antonio Gramsci con altre lettere di Piero Sraffa*, ed. Antonio A. Santucci, with a preface by Nicolà Badaloni, Rome: Riuniti, 1986.

Harcourt, Geoffrey C. : 'An early Post-Keynesian: Lorie Tarshis (or: Tarshis on Tarshis by Harcourt)', *Journal of Post-Keynesian Economics*, Vol. IV, No. 4, summer 1982, pp. 609–19.

Harrod, Roy F. : 'Review of *Production of Commodities by Means of Commodities*', *Economic Journal*, Vol. LXXI, December 1961, pp. 783–87.

Hayek, Friedrich August von: 'Money and Capital: a reply', *Economic Journal*, vol. XLII, June 1932, pp. 237–49.

Heertje, Arnold: 'On Discovering a Second "Freak" Copy of Ricardo's *Principles* and the Say Archives', *History of Economics Society Bulletin* (Nashville, Tenn.,), Vol. 10, No. 1, spring 1988, pp. 75–6.

Hession, Charles H. : *John Maynard Keynes: A Personal Biography of the Man who Revolutionized Capitalism and the Way we Live*, New York: Macmillan, 1983.

Iotti, Nilde: 'Nascose ai fascisti i *Quaderni del Carcere*' (Raffaele Mattioli) *Rinascita* (Rome), No. 31, 3 August 1973, p. 21.

Jannaccone, Pasquale: 'Scienza, critica e realtà economica', *La Riforma Sociale*, 37th year, Vol. XLI, No. 11–12, November–December 1930, pp. 521–28.

Kahn, Richard Ferdinand: *The Economics of the Short Period* (doctoral theses, Cambridge, 1929), London: Macmillan, 1989.

—— *The Making of Keynes' General Theory: Raffaele Mattioli Lectures*, Cambridge: Cambridge University Press, 1984.

Kaldor, Nicholas: 'Piero Sraffa' (read on the occasion of a remembrance ceremony, Cambridge, September 1983), *Cambridge Journal of Economics*, Vol. 8, No. 1, March 1984, pp. 1–5.

—— 'Piero Sraffa (1898–1983)', *Proceedings of the British Academy*, Cardiff: Oxford University Press, Vol. LXXI, 1985, pp. 615–40.

Keynes, John Maynard: *A Treatise on Money, The Collected Writings*, London: Macmillan and Cambridge University Press, Vols. V and VI, 1971.

—— *Essays in Biography, The Collected Writings* London: Macmillan and Cambridge University Press, Vol. X, 1972.

—— *The General Theory of Employment, Interest and Money, The Collected Writings*, London: Macmillan and Cambridge University Press, Vol. VII, 1973.

—— *The General Theory and After*, Part I, *Preparation, The Collected Writings*, London: Macmillan and Cambridge University Press, Vol. XIII, 1973.

—— *The General Theory and After: a Supplement, The Collected Writings*, London: Macmillan and New York: Cambridge University Press, Vol. XXIX, 1979.

—— *Activities, 1920–1922: Treaty Revision and Reconstruction, The Collected Writings*, London: Macmillan and Cambridge University Press, Vol. XVII, 1977.

—— *Activities, 1929–1931: Rethinking Employment and Unemployment Policies, The Collected Writings*, London: Macmillan and New York: Cambridge University Press, Vol. XX 1981.

—— *Activities, 1939–1945: Internal War Finance, The Collected Writings*, London: Macmillan and New York: Cambridge University Press, Vol. XXII, 1978.

—— *Activities, 1940–1944: Shaping the Post-war World: the Clearing Union, The Collected Writings*, London: Macmillan and New York: Cambridge University Press, Vol. XXV, 1980.

—— *Social, Political and Literary Writings, The Collected Writings*, London: Macmillan and New York: Cambridge University Press, Vol. XXVIII, 1982.

Keynes, Milo, ed. *Essays on John Maynard Keynes*, Cambridge: Cambridge University Press, 1975.

Labriola, Antonio: 'Lettere a F. Engels', 28 October 1892 and 16 August 1894, *Lo Stato Operaio* (Paris), 3rd year, No. 2, February 1929, pp. 147–56, No. 7, September–October 1929, pp. 616–24.

—— *Scritti filosofici e politici*, ed. Sbarberi, Turin: Einaudi, 1973, 2 vols.

Lenti, Libero: 'Gli ottant' anni della Bocconi' *Nuova Antologia* (Florence), 118th year, Vol. 552, fasc. 2148, October–December 1983, pp. 205–49.

Lisa, Athos: *Memorie: In carcere con Gramsci*, Milan: Feltrinelli, 1973.

Macchioro, Aurelio: 'A proposito di una collana ISEDI di classici del pensiero economico', *Storia del Pensiero Economico: Bollettino di Informazione* (Florence), No. 1, March 1973, pp. 12–19.

Macciocchi, Maria-Antonietta: *Pour Gramsci*, Paris: Le Seuil, 1974.

Maione, Giuseppe: *Il biennio rosso: Autonomia e spontaneità operaia nel 1919–1920*, Bologna: Il Mulino, 1975.

Malagodi, Giovanni: *Profilo di Raffaele Mattioli*, Milan and Naples: Riccardo Ricciardi (published privately), 1984.

Marshall, Alfred: *Principles of Economics*, 8th edition (1920), London: Macmillan, reprinted 1959.

Meek, Ronald L. : *Economics and Ideology and other Essays: Studies in the Development of Economic Thought*, London: Chapman and Hall, 1967.

Meldolesi, Luca: 'Piero Sraffa, il percorso di un' analisi e di una cultura e vicenda morale e mentale di un comunista degli anni' 20, da Marx a Ricardo (e St Simon)', *Il Manifesto* (Rome), 6 June 1980, p. 3.

—— *L'utopia realmente esistente: Marx e Saint-Simon*, (with an appendix, 'Piero Sraffa e il marxismo'), Bari: Laterza, 1982.

Ministero della Pubblica Istruzione, 'Relazione della commissione giudicatrice del concorso per professore non stabile alla cattedra di economia politica nella R. università di Cagliari', *Bollettino Ufficiale*, Part II, *Atti di Amministrazione*, Rome, 53rd year, Vol. I, No. 9, 4 March 1926, pp. 773–7.

Morandi, Rodolfo: 'Lettere a Pietro Ernandez (1927–1953)', ed. Aldo Agosti, preface by Eugenio Pennatti, *Annali della Fondazione Luigi Einaudi* (Turin), Vol. III, 1969, pp. 227–495.

Mossa, Lorenzo: 'Angelo Sraffa', *Rivista del Diritto Commerciale e del Diritto Generale delle Obbligazioni* (Milan), Vol. XXXVI, Part I, fasc. 1, 1938, pp. 7–18.

Napoleoni, Claudio: 'Sulla teoria della produzione come processo circolare', *Giornale degli Economisti e Annali di Economia* (Padua), Vol. XX, January–February 1961, pp. 101–17.

Napolitano, Giorgio: 'La "vita segreta" di un grande intellectuale' (read on the occasion of a remembrance ceremony, Rome, 25 October 1983), *Rinascita* (Rome), No. 42, 28 October 1983, pp.34–5.

Newman, Peter K. : 'Production of Commodities by Means of Commodities', *Schweizerische Zeitschrift für Volkswirtschaft und Statistik: Revue suisse d'économie politique et de statistique*, Vol. XCVIII, March 1962, pp. 58–75.

Ormea, Ferdinando: *Le origini dello stalinismo nel P. C. I. : Storia della 'svolta' comunista degli anni Trenta*, Milan: Feltrinelli, 1978.

Panico, Carlo: 'Sraffa on Money and Banking', *Cambridge Journal of Economics*, Vol. 12, No. 1, March 1988, pp. 7–28.

Pasinetti, Luigi L. : 'Sraffa, Piero', in *International Encyclopedia of the Social Sciences: Biographical Supplement*, Vol. 18, New York: Free Press, 1979, pp. 736–8; Italian edition enlarged: 'Piero Sraffa (1898–1983): breve saggio bio-bibliografico', *Economia Politica: Rivista di teoria e analisi* (Bologna), 2nd year, No. 3, December 1985, pp. 333–41.

Patinkin, Don, and Leith, J. Clark: *Keynes, Cambridge and the General Theory: The Process of Criticism and Discussion Connected with the Development of the General Theory*, London: Macmillan, 1977.

Paulesu Quercioli, Mimma, ed. : *Gramsci vivo nelle testimonianze dei suoi contemporanei*, Milan: Feltrinelli, 1977.

Pollitt, Brian H. : 'The Collaboration of Maurice Dobb in Sraffa's Edition of Ricardo', *Cambridge Journal of Economics*, Vol. 12, No. 1, March 1988, pp. 55–65.

Porta, Pier Luigi: 'Piero Sraffa (1898–1983)', *Rivista Internazionale di Science Economiche e Commerciali* (Milan), 31st year, No. 1, January 1984, pp. 14–20.

—— 'How Piero Sraffa took up the Editorship of David Ricardo's *Works and Correspondence*, *History of Economics Society Bulletin* (Nashville, Tenn.), Vol. VIII, No. 1, summer 1986, pp. 35–7.

Potier, Jean-Pierre: *Lectures italiennes de Marx: Les conflits d' interprétation che les économistes et les philosophes (1883–1983)*, Lyon: Presses Universitaires de Lyon, 1986.

Ranchetti, Fabio: 'Mattioli "economista critico"', *Rivista di Storia Economica* (Venice), new series, Vol. III, No. 2, June 1986, pp. 229–36 .

Ravera, Camilla: *Diario di trent' anni: 1913–1943*, Rome: Riuniti, 1973.

Robertson, Dennis H. : 'Some Notes on Mr Keynes's General Theory of Employment', *Quarterly Journal of Economics*, vol. LI, November 1936, pp. 168–91.

—— *Essays in Monetary Theory*, London: King, 1940.

Robinson, Joan: *The Economics of Imperfect Competition*, London: Macmillan, 1933.

—— *Economic Heresies: some Old-Fashioned Questions in Economic Theory*, London: Macmillan, 1971.

—— *Contributions to Modern Economics*, Oxford: Basil Blackwell, 1978.

—— 'Prelude to a Critique of Economic Theory', *Oxford Economic Papers*, new series, Vol. XIII, February 1961, pp. 53–8.

Roncaglia, Alessandro: *Sraffa e la teoria dei prezzi*, Bari: Laterza, 1975, second edition, with an appendix, 'La rivoluzione di Sraffa', 1981; English translation of the first edition, *Sraffa and the Theory of Prices*, Chichester, Wiley, 1978.

—— 'Piero Sraffa: una bibliografia ragionata', *Studi Economici* (Naples), 38th year, No. 21, 1983, pp. 137–66.

—— 'Sraffa e le banche', *Rivista Milanese di Economia* (Milan), No. 10, April–June, 1984, pp. 104–12.

—— 'In redazione o in pizzeria', in *Cento anni Latersa (1885–1985): Testimonianze degli autori*, Bari: Laterza, 1986, pp. 212–13.

Rosselli, Carlo: *Epistolario familiare: Carlo, Nello Rosselli e la madre, 1914–1937*, ed. Zeffiro Ciuffoletti, introduction by Leo Valiani, Milan: Sugarco, 1979.

Schumpeter, Joseph-Alois, *Ten Great Economists: From Marx to Keynes*, New York: Oxford University Press, 1951.

Secrest, Meryle: *Being Bernard Berenson: A Critical Biography*, New York: Holt Rinehart and Winston, 1979.

Skidelsky, Robert: *John Maynard Keynes: A Biography*, Vol. 1, *Hopes Betrayed, 1883–1920*, London: Macmillan, 1983.

—— 'Keynes and Sraffa: a Problem of Non-communication', Italian translation, 'Keynes e Sraffa: un caso di non-communicazione', in Riccardo Bellofiore, ed. *Tra teoria economica e grande cultura europea: Piero Sraffa*, Milan: Franco Angeli, 1986, pp. 73–84.

Sorel, Georges: *Lettere a Benedetto Croce*, Bari: Laterza, 1980.

Spriano, Paolo: *L'occupazione delle fabbriche*, Turin: Einaudi, 1968.

—— 'Gli ultimi anni di Gramsci in un colloquio con Piero Sraffa', *Rinascita* (Rome), No. 15, 14 April 1967, pp. 14–16.

—— *Storia del Partito Comunista Italiano*, Turin: Einaudi, Vol. 3, *I Fronti Popolari, Stalin, la guerra*, 1970.

—— *Gramsci in carcere e il partito*, Rome: Riuniti, 1977; 2nd edition, 1988.

—— 'L'altra metà di Gramsci', *L'Unità* (Rome), 6 September 1983, p. 9.

Sraffa, Piero: 'L'inflazione monetaria in Italia durante e dopo la guerra', doctoral thesis, University of Turin, 1920.
—— 'Open Shop Drive', *L'Ordine Nuovo* (Turin), 2 series, 5 July 1921, p. 3.
—— 'Industriali e governo inglese contro i lavoratori', *L'Ordine Nuovo* (Turin), 2 series, 24 July 1921, p. 3.
—— 'I "Labour leaders"', *L'Ordine Nuovo* (Turin), 2 series, 4 August 1921, pp. 1–2.
—— 'The Bank Crisis in Italy', *Economic Journal*, Vol. XXXII, June 1922, pp. 178–97.
—— 'Italian Banking Today', *Manchester Guardian Commercial: Reconstruction in Europe*, Supplement No. XI, 7 December 1922, pp. 675–6.
—— 'Opinioni', *La Rivoluzione Liberale* (Turin), 2nd year, No. 31, 16 October 1923, p. 128.
—— 'Obituary: Maffeo Pantaleoni', *Economic Journal*, Vol. XXXIV, December 1924, pp. 648–53.
—— 'Sulle relazioni fra costo e quantità prodotta', *Annali di Economia* (Milan), Vol. II, 1925, pp. 277–328; reprinted in *Saggi*, Bologna: Il Mulino, 1986, pp. 15–65.
—— 'The Laws of Returns under Competitive Conditions', *Economic Journal*, vol. XXXVI, December 1926, pp. 535–50.
—— and Tasca, Angelo: 'Polemica monetaria', *Lo Stato Operaio* (Paris), 1st year, No. 9–10, November–December 1927, pp. 1089–95, reprinted under the title 'Il vero significato della "quota novanta"', in Lucio Villari, ed. *Il capitalismo italiano del Novecento*, Bari: Laterza, 1975, Vol. I, pp. 180–91.
—— 'A Criticism' and 'A Rejoinder', in 'Increasing Returns and the Representative Firm', *Economic Journal*, Vol. XL, March 1930, pp. 89–92 and 93.
—— 'An Alleged Correction of Ricardo', *Quarterly Journal of Economics*, Vol. XLIV, May 1930, pp. 539–44.
—— 'Dr Hayek on Money and Capital', *Economic Journal*, Vol. XLII, March 1932, pp. 42–53.
—— 'A Rejoinder', *Economic Journal*, Vol. XLII, June 1932, pp. 249–51.
—— 'General Preface' and 'Introduction', in David Ricardo, *On the Principles of Political Economy and Taxation, The Works and Correspondence*, Cambridge: Cambridge University press, Vol. I, 1951, pp. vii-xi and xiii-lxii.
—— 'Addenda to the Memoir of Ricardo', 'Ricardo in Business', 'A Survey of Ricardo Manuscripts', in David Ricardo: *Biographical Miscellany, The Works and Correspondence*, Cambridge: Cambridge University Press, Vol. X, 1955, pp. 16–64, 65–106 and 386–92.
—— *Production of Commodities by Means of Commodities: Prelude to a Critique of Economic Theory*, Cambridge: Cambridge University Press, 1960; Italian edition, *Produzione di merci a mezzo di merci: Premesse a una critica della teoria economica*, Turin: Einaudi, 1960.
—— 'Production of Commodities: a Comment', *Economic Journal*, Vol. LXXII, June 1962, pp. 477–9.
—— *Ecrits d'économie politique*, French translation and introduction by Gilbert Faccarello, preface by Gilbert Abraham-Frois, Paris: Economica, 1975.
—— *Saggi*, notice by Pierangelo Garegnani and foreword by the editor, Bologna: Il Mulino, 1986.
—— letter dated February or March 1924, partly published, ed. Antonio Gramsci, in 'Problemi di oggi e di domani', *L'Ordine Nuovo*, 3 series, No. 3–4, 1–15 April 1924, reprinted in Gramsci: *La costruzione del Partito Comunista*, Turin: Einaudi, 1971, pp. 175–81.

—— letter to Angelo Tasca, 22 September 1927, *Rinascita* (Rome), No. 31, 4 August 1978, pp. 24–5, reprinted in *Rinascita*, No. 35, 9 September 1983, p. 26.

—— letter to J. M. Keynes, 6 June 1926, partly published in Alessandro Roncaglia: *Sraffa and the Theory of Prices*, Chichester: Wiley, 1978, pp. 11–13.

—— letter to Giulio Einaudi, 30 November 1948, photograph in *Cinquant' anni di un editore: Le Edizioni Einaudi negli anni 1933–1983*, Turin: Einaudi, 1983.

—— letter to Luigi Einaudi on physiocracy, 22 August 1958, *Political Economy: Studies in the Surplus Approach* (Turin), Vol. 4, No. 1, 1988, pp. 153–5.

—— letters to Peter K. Newman, 4 and 19 June 1962, ed. Krishna Bharadwaj, in 'On the Maximum Number of Switches between two Production Systems', appendix, *Schweizerische Zeitschrift für Volkswirtschaft und Statistik: Revue suisse d'économie politique et de statistique*, Vol. CVI, December 1970, pp. 424–8.

—— unpublished letters: to Luigi Einaudi (1921–61), preserved at the Fondazione Luigi Einaudi (Turin); to Angelo Tasca (1927–30), preserved at the Fondazione GianGiacomo Feltrinelli (Milan); to Tatiana Schucht (1929–38), preserved at the Fondazione Gramsci (Rome); to Joseph A. Schumpeter, 8 May 1930, preserved in the Schumpeter Papers, Harvard University Archives, Cambridge, Mass.

Staehle, Hans: 'La Réunion de la Société d'Économétrie, Lausanne, Septembre 1931', *Econometrica*, Vol. 1, 1933, pp. 73–86.

Tasca, Angelo: 'La rivalutazione della lira e la crisi della economia italiana', *Lo Stato Operaio* (Paris), 1st year, No. 6, August 1927, pp. 667–92.

Togliatti, Palmiro: *Lezioni sul fascismo*, Rome: Riuniti, 1970; English translation, *Lectures on Fascism*, London: Lawrence & Wishart, 1976.

—— *La formazione del gruppo dirigente del P. C. I. nel 1923–1924*, Rome: Riuniti, 1962.

Tranfaglia, Nicolà: *Carlo Rosselli dall' interventismo a 'Giustizia e Libertà'*, Bari: Laterza, 1968.

Turati, Filippo, and Kuliscioff, Anna: *Carteggio*, Vol. VI, *1923–1925, Il delitto Matteotti e l'Aventino*, collected by Alessandro Schiavi, ed. Franco Pedone, Turin: Einaudi, 1977 .

Weatherall, David: *David Ricardo: A Biography*, The Hague: Nijhoff, 1976.

Whitaker, John K., ed.: *The Early Economic Writings of Alfred Marshall, 1867–1890*, London: Macmillan, Vol. 1, 1975.

Wittgenstein, Ludwig: *Philosophical Investigations*, 3rd edition, New York: Macmillan, 1958.

Wright, Georg-Henrik von: 'Biographical Sketch', in Norman Malcolm: *Ludwig Wittgenstein: A Memoir*, London: Oxford University Press, 1958.

Zanni, Alberto: 'Sulla mancata apparizione della "Teoria generale" di Keynes in una seconda serie della "Nuova collana di economisti" (con corrispondenze inediti)', *Quaderni di Storia dell' Economia Politica* (Milan), 3rd year, No. 3, 1985, pp. 253–75.

Name index